Thomas Pointon Dale

**The History of Brunswick Church, Bury**

Thomas Pointon Dale

**The History of Brunswick Church, Bury**

ISBN/EAN: 9783337162184

Printed in Europe, USA, Canada, Australia, Japan

Cover: Foto ©ninafisch / pixelio.de

More available books at **www.hansebooks.com**

# THE

# HISTORY

OF

# BRUNSWICK

# CHURCH,

BURY.

BY

THOMAS POINTON DALE.

BURY:

E. W. B. SMITH, HAYMARKET STREET;

FLETCHER & SPEIGHT, SILVER STREET.

LONDON:

SIMPKIN, MARSHALL, HAMILTON, KENT & CO., LIMITED.

1896.

TO THE YOUNGER MEMBERS

OF THE

BRUNSWICK CONGREGATION,

THIS VOLUME

𝔍𝔰 𝔄𝔣𝔣𝔢𝔠𝔱𝔦𝔬𝔫𝔞𝔱𝔢𝔩𝔶 𝔍𝔫𝔰𝔠𝔯𝔦𝔟𝔢𝔡,

IN THE HOPE THAT

A DOUBLE PORTION OF THE SPIRIT OF THEIR FATHERS

MAY BE UPON THEM.

# PREFACE.

THIS work was undertaken at the request of the annual meeting of the Church whose history it relates. Few persons are now living who can remember the events which led to the formation of Brunswick Church sixty years ago, and it was felt that if any advantage was to be gained from their recollections it must be secured without delay. The writer's five years' residence as a circuit minister in Bury was supposed to have given him some qualification for the task.

The book was commenced in the early part of the present year, and has been written amidst the inevitable engagements of a Methodist minister's life. This fact may be pleaded in excuse for any omissions or blunders which may hereafter be discovered. As far as possible old documents and minute books have been consulted, and the magazines of the denomination have been diligently searched for reports and biographies.

One omission may be at once remedied. In the account of the Hacking family in Chapter iii., no mention is made of Hannah, the younger daughter of Joseph Hacking, who became the wife of Mr. John Stockdale. She was a bright and intelligent woman, generous and kind to the poor, and deeply interested in the work of the Church. For many years she was secretary to the Dorcas Society. Her death took place while on a visit to her friends in Bury, in August, 1893.

The writer has had the assistance of a small committee, who were appointed with him to read the proof-sheets. The committee consisted of Messrs. L. FLETCHER, J. K. LORD, J. H. RILEY, J. HOLT, E. W. B. SMITH, and I. INGHAM.

It is worthy of note that this book has been produced almost entirely by members of the executive body of the Church. The author, printer, photographer, and publisher all belong to the Brunswick Leaders' Meeting.

The illustrations and portraits, with two exceptions, are from photographs by Messrs. E. Eccles and Sons, of Bury and Bacup. The portrait of Joseph Hacking is from an original oil-painting, and that of the Rev. W. R. Sunman from a print kindly supplied by that gentleman. In the selection of the portraits the committee have exercised much thought and discrimination. Six out of the seven smaller ones that are printed in the text are from photographs now hanging in the Sunday School, that of William Robinson being added by special desire. No justification is needed for the inclusion of those of the earlier ministers, nor for that of Joseph Hacking, the father of the late Rev. Thomas Hacking. The Rev. John Mather is the oldest surviving minister, and the Rev. W. R. Sunman is President of the U.M.F.C. for the year now closing. Efforts have been made to obtain portraits of James Livesey, John Lord, and John Ashworth, but without avail.

It is believed that this is the first attempt to give a detailed history of any Church in the denomination, or of any place of worship in the town of Bury.

*July 6th, 1896.*

# CONTENTS.

CONTENTS.

## CHAPTER IV.

### THE OLD CHAPEL.

## CHAPTER V.

### EARLY PROGRESS.

## CHAPTER VI.

### EARLY PROGRESS (continued).

## CHAPTER VII.

### " LET US RISE AND BUILD."

## CHAPTER VIII.

### THE NEW CHAPEL.

## CHAPTER IX.

### RECENT TIMES.

## APPENDICES.

# LIST OF ILLUSTRATIONS.

# HISTORY OF BRUNSWICK CHURCH.

## CHAPTER I.

### THE RISE OF FREE METHODISM.

" Some men, and some good men too perhaps, fret, and out of their own weakness are in agony, lest these divisions and sub-divisions will undo us. The adversary again applauds, and waits the hour. . . . Fool ! he sees not the firm root, out of which we all grow, though into branches."

MILTON : *Areopagitica.*

THE history of Brunswick Church cannot well be written without some attempt to describe the origin of the religious denomination to which it belongs. We are so far removed from the events here narrated, that this may surely be done without prejudice. The echoes of the controversies which agitated the Wesleyan Methodist Connexion during the second quarter of the present century,

have now almost died away, but the results still
remain, in the existence of the body known as the.
United Methodist Free Churches. The many
divisions of Methodism are somewhat bewildering
to outsiders, who are apt to wonder why people
professing the same religious beliefs, and worshipping
in much the same fashion, should yet maintain their
separate and distinct organisations. In setting forth
the origin of one of them, I would endeavour to do
so as a historical fact, and in the hope that no word
here written will retard, even for a moment, the
approach of the day when, if it be possible, all
shall again become one.

It is necessary, however, to justify our fathers in
the course they took of severing the ties of
ecclesiastical kinship, and leaving the Church to
which they owed their best life. Christian men do
not take such a step with a light heart. The
character of the founders of Brunswick Chapel is
above the suspicion that they were moved by
personal discontent or ambition. They, at least,
felt that there was serious reason for their action;

nor did they stand alone. There must have been something radically defective in the policy of Wesleyan Methodism, which made it subject to the convulsions by which it was shaken during a period of more than fifty years, from 1797 to 1849. Catastrophies do not occur without cause, and the recent changes that have been made in the constitution of that body, go to prove that there was some reason for the dissatisfaction which then existed.

John Wesley died in 1791. After his death certain questions, such as the administration of the Sacraments, and the power to be accorded to the laity, which his personal ascendency had kept in abeyance, came up for discussion. The Conference of 1795 formulated a " Plan of Pacification," with the object of remedying some defects in the constitution of the body, and of conferring important privileges upon the societies, which they had not hitherto enjoyed. That this measure did not give entire satisfaction, is evident from the disruption of 1797, which resulted in the formation of the Methodist New Connexion. The

Conference of that year further extended the "Plan of Pacification," by what are known as the "Leeds Concessions," which were embodied in a printed circular and distributed among the societies. One of these concessions was that "no regulations will be finally confirmed till after a year's consideration, and the knowledge of the sentiments of the Connexion at large [has been obtained], through the medium of all their public officers." It was also provided that "no person must be expelled from the society for any breach of our rules, or even for manifest immorality, till such fact or crime has been proved at a leaders' meeting."

Had these concessions been remembered and observed, British Methodism might have had a happier history, and many years of agitation and division been spared.

At the Conference of 1834, it was proposed to establish a theological institute for the training of ministers, and the proposal was carried, and put into effect forthwith. Many devout and intelligent Methodists of that period were conscientiously opposed to the idea of a training college. They believed that if men were called of God to the work, and had given evidence of their call by their success as local preachers, the Holy Spirit would enable them to equip themselves for the larger ministry. They feared, too, that a college would tend to develop a spirit of professionalism, and though it might produce a more learned ministry; yet would be liable to neutralize the natural endowments of the men, and diminish their spiritual power. No one would venture to make such objections to-day. Experience has shown that the advantages of a systematic training far outweigh the possible evils. A generation which has recognised the value of technical instruction in all branches of art and industry, would not be likely to withhold it from the Christian ministry. But the old-fashioned views were then so common and so widespread as to render it highly inexpedient for the Conference to ignore them.

The chief objection, however, to the action of the Conference, was not the institution itself, but the

manner in which the proposal was made. In face of
the concession of 1797, to give a year's consideration
to new regulations in order to gain "a knowledge of
the sentiments of the Connexion at large," the
scheme was introduced and agreed to by the
ministers assembled, and no attempt was made to
secure the consent or co-operation of the members.
To many this method of procedure seemed both
unconstitutional and despotic. There was a growing feeling of distrust and suspicion towards the
Conference. Six years previously, in 1828, the
Conference had consented to the erection of an
organ in Brunswick Chapel, Leeds, in opposition
to the wishes of the members, as expressed by a
majority of sixty votes to one in their leaders'
meeting, and which resulted in the secession of a
thousand members, and the formation of a body
known for a while as the Protestant Methodists.

The spirit of the age was making men restive
under all forms, or supposed forms, of despotism.
It was the period of the first Reform Bill, the birth-
day of democratic government in the state ; and the

Wesleyan Conference would have been wise to have discerned the signs of the times, and not have chosen this as the hour in which to turn its back upon the liberal concessions of 1797.

The Conference of 1834 was followed by meetings of those who dissented from its action, and, shortly after, they formed a "Grand Central Association," their aims being to stimulate public opinion and to induce the Conference to modify its claims. The demands formulated by the Association were extremely moderate. They asked for a re-statement of the Rules of 1797, and for the admission of the people to a share in Church government; but their proposals were treated with contempt; the leaders of the movement were expelled from membership, and hosts of sympathizers suffered with them. The dissentients assembled at Sheffield, during the sittings of the Conference in the following year, and endeavoured in vain to present their case. All hope of reconciliation was abandoned, and the Wesleyan Association was thereupon established as a separate and distinct Methodist organisation. The extent of

the loss to Wesleyan Methodism cannot be fully
estimated, but the first statistics of the new denomination, presented at their Annual Assembly in 1837,
showed a membership of over 21,000.

The reactionary policy adopted by the Conference,
besides provoking the division just described also
laid the train for the still greater convulsion
which followed in 1849. It is beyond my purpose
to describe the movement which brought about the
expulsion of Everett, Dunn, and Griffith, and resulted
in the formation of the body known as the Wesleyan
Reformers. Bury Methodism had already lost
some of its most liberal-minded supporters, so this
movement had here, as at other places in the vicinity,
little or no material left to work upon. The Reformers
eventually amalgamated with the Association, and
formed, at Rochdale, in 1857, the United Methodist
Free Churches.

Free Methodism has grown out of the principles
which were advocated by these Reformers. Its form
of government is democratic, and combines circuit
independence with connexional unity. Its polity and

doctrinal basis are set forth in legal form in a Foundation Deed. This deed defines the constitution of the Annual Assembly, which must be composed of the freely elected representatives of the circuits, who may be either ministers or laymen. The Assembly is empowered to deal with itinerant ministers, and to appoint them to their circuits. In the circuits the highest court is the Quarterly Meeting, which in internal matters is practically self-governing. The doctrinal statement, which prescribes the truths to be preached in the chapels belonging to the denomination, is concise and comprehensive. It is similar to that of other Methodist bodies, and claims to be scriptural and evangelical.

As a religious body it has made considerable' progress. At the Annual Assembly of 1895 it reported over 80,000 church members, and its adherents will number at least three times as many.

# CHAPTER II.

## THE BEGINNINGS OF FREE METHODISM IN BURY.

"From the whole tenor of the several texts wherein the word 'schism' occurs, it is manifest that it is not separation *from* any church, but a separation *in* a church."

JOHN WESLEY.

ANCHESTER was the chief centre of the agitation described in the previous chapter. The Rev. Samuel Warren, LL.D., superintendent minister of the Oldham Street Circuit, in that city, was suspended from the duties of his office for writing a pamphlet, containing strictures on the proposed theological institute, and the manner in which it had been imposed upon the Connexion.

The Manchester papers of that period gave lengthy reports of the proceedings, and of the crowded and excited meetings which were held in consequence. Judging by these reports, and the

editorial comments upon them, it would seem that
public sympathy outside the denomination was
almost entirely on the side of the reformers. The
movement rapidly spread to the surrounding districts,
and extended to many parts of the country. The
strong and wealthy Rochdale Circuit went almost
wholly against the Conference, and at a meeting of
stewards, leaders, and local preachers, it was
unanimously resolved to join hand and heart with
the Manchester Methodists' Association.

The first account of the agitation in Bury is a
report in a periodical called *The Watchman's Lantern*,
of "a most respectable meeting," which was held
on April 10th, 1835, in the Methodist New Connexion Chapel, Bolton Street. Mr. James Livesey
conducted the devotional exercises, and the meeting
was addressed by Dr. Warren, and other gentlemen
from Manchester and Liverpool. The meeting
lasted from three to four hours, and the "deepest
attention was evinced by a crowded audience." At
the close a resolution was unanimously adopted, on
the motion of Mr. D. Rowland, of Liverpool,

seconded by Mr. John Robinson Kay, of Bury, cordially approving of the objects of the Association, and solemnly pledging the meeting to a zealous co-operation therewith.

In the same month, a large number of delegates from various towns assembled in a spacious wooden erection, called " The Tabernacle," in Stevenson Square, Manchester, for the purpose of discussing the ecclesiastical situation, and of securing united action in the plan of reform which it was proposed to submit to the ensuing Wesleyan Conference. Bury was represented at that meeting by three gentlemen whose names are famous in local Methodism—James Livesey, John Robinson Kay, and John Lord. Nothing was further from the minds of the reformers than the idea of separation from the parent body. They were only desirous of obtaining such alterations in the constitution as they believed would secure for the people a fair share of power in the legislation and administration of the Connexion, and thus prevent further encroachments upon their liberties. But the Conference of that day was, as

we have seen, quite content with things as they
were. It met the agitation by a policy of repression.
Many of the reformers who held official positions
were summarily suspended, and those who sym-
pathized with them were, in many cases, expelled
from membership.

There happened to be in Bury a superintendent
minister whose antipathy towards the friends of the
Association was very pronounced. It was publicly
reported that in his zeal he had expelled John
Robinson Kay, one of the most liberal and active
supporters of the cause, for circulating the "affectionate address" of the Wesleyan Association. The
report was probably unfounded, for the family of
Robinson Kay have been closely identified with
Wesleyan Methodism in this district unto this day.
It is, however, certain that his sympathies were with
the reformers, and that he played a leading part in
the earlier stages of the movement.

The first and most notable withdrawal that took
place in Bury was that of James Livesey. This
venerable man had been for fifty years a member of

society, forty years a local preacher and leader, and was a trustee for every chapel in the circuit. He was brought to trial at the leaders' meeting on the charge of presiding at an Association meeting in Rochdale. The reformers of that town, who comprised nearly all the officials of the circuit, had arranged for a meeting in their principal chapel, in order to ventilate their grievances. The doors were locked against them, so they took refuge in two Nonconformist chapels, which were generously placed at their disposal. The meeting at which James Livesey presided was held in the large Baptist Chapel in West Street, which was crowded, and his speech as chairman was a careful and temperate utterance. This was the offence preferred against him at the leaders' meeting. The superintendent deferred judgment for seven days, although he was urged by those present to end the case at once; whereupon Livesey gave up his class book, saying that "he was determined not to walk the streets of Bury with the sentence hanging over his head."

The following week, on October 17th, 1835, a

meeting was held in Bethel Independent Chapel,
Henry Street, to express sympathy with Livesey,
and to pledge its support to him and to any other
officer or member of the circuit who might be called
upon to suffer in like manner.   The meeting
further took into consideration the "measures to
be adopted in the present agitated state of the
society."   What "measures" were adopted will be
seen in due course.

Meanwhile, another cause was at work, which,
added to that already explained, brought about the
division which resulted in the establishment of Bury
Free Methodism.   The Sunday School had grown
up, largely, as a distinct and separate organisation
from the Church.   It managed its own affairs, elected
its own officers and committee, controlled its own
funds, and regulated its own methods of teaching.
It was, to all intents and purposes, an independent
and self-governing institution.   The Conference of
1827, in its wisdom, drew up certain general rules
and regulations, for the purpose of bringing the
Sunday schools under connexional discipline and

control. New schools were required to comply with these rules, and existing schools were urged to do so. They were, in future, to be denominated Wesleyan Methodist Sunday Schools. The superintendent minister was placed in a position of authority; the constitution of the committee was to be restricted,—three-fourths of the members thereof to be elected from outside the body of teachers,—and every teacher was either to be a member of society, or to be approved at a leaders' meeting; school premises were to be legally secured to the trustees of the nearest chapel; and it was prohibited to teach writing on the Sunday.

It will readily be seen that the imposition of these rules upon many schools would amount to a revolution. It was felt to be so in Bury, Rochdale, and other places where large Sunday schools existed. Possibly, under other circumstances, and after reasonable persuasion, the new regulations might, in course of time, have been submitted to. But so great was the resentment against the proceedings of the Conference in other matters, that when the

C

proposed reforms were attempted to be enforced, the most stern and uncompromising opposition was provoked.

One Sunday morning, the scholars and teachers assembled in Clerke Street School, according to custom. The hour at length arrived for adjournment to the chapel in Union Street, for Divine worship. The procession, however, took a different direction. Some few elected to go to the chapel as usual, but the large majority proceeded along Clough Street, Stanley Street, and John Street, and finally entered a building that had been used as a woollen warehouse, belonging to Messrs. Harrison, in Paradise Street. There they found a room provided for their reception, where they united together in worship, and until the chapel in North Street was built, that continued to be their meeting place.

There is no record as to the precise time at which this incident occurred. The earliest written date is January 10th, 1836, when a collection was taken at

the room in Paradise Street, and which amounted to
£23 4s. 6¾d.

On January 17th it was resolved—

"That all the teachers that are dissatisfied with the
Conference plan of teaching the scholars, do withdraw from
the old school, and commence a new one in Paradise Street,
on Sunday, January ——, 1836."

The extent of the secession may be gathered from
the fact that there were 176 teachers and 863
scholars in the new school, which was, in point of
numbers, the largest in the town; also, that when
the statistics of the society were first collected, in
the April following, it comprised 278 members.

An appeal was made for public support, and the
following address, written by Joseph Hacking, was
printed and circulated :

"We, the Teachers of the Sunday School now established
in Paradise Street, Bury, wish to call the attention of our
friends and the public in general, to our present situation.
It is now nearly fifty years since we first commenced, by
gratuitous services, a Sunday School in Clerke Street, at a
time when no other School was in being, except one belonging to the Establishment, whose Teachers were paid for
their services. We have the satisfaction to say, that

thousands who are now heads of families in the town and neighbourhood, have passed through our school, and have reaped from it considerable advantages ; and we presume that under Divine Providence, we have been the means of exciting in other denominations of our Christian Brethren a laudable emulation, in attempting by free labour, to promote the welfare of the rising generation. By the constant and kind support of our friends, we have been enabled to the present, to supply the wants of from 800 to 1,000 children, annually, with Premises, Books, and every other accommodation, as thousands who have benefited thereby can bear ample witness.

" But while thus earnestly and sincerely labouring to promote the public good, our services have been attempted to be fettered, by taking from us the management of our own labours, and of the finances entrusted to our care, so as in a great measure to nullify and render our means inefficient for the purposes to which they have hitherto been directed. We have therefore, to preserve our own freedom and to render our labours energetic and efficient as heretofore, been compelled to take other premises, and to supply them with *new forms, desks, books*, and other *accommodations*, being now 176 Teachers and having under our immediate care 863 children ; the expenses attending which, it will be evident, must be very considerable."

It is unnecessary to dwell at greater length upon events which must have been of painful interest at

the time they occurred.  Enough has been said to
explain the causes of the secession, and to justify
the establishment of a new religious denomination
in Bury.  The history of Brunswick Church and
School proves that there was abundant scope for
the various energies which it has called into exercise
for the space of sixty years.  The Wesleyan body
has to a large extent recovered itself from the
losses which it then sustained.  The two churches
have learnt to respect and love each other for their
work's sake.  They dwell side by side, in mutual
friendliness; in that unity of the spirit which is
better than unity of organisation, and which is the
bond of peace.  The points on which they agree
are far more numerous and more important than
those on which they differ.  The differences are
entirely those of polity and organisation; in their
doctrinal beliefs, in their religious usages and modes
of worship, they are one.

# CHAPTER III.

## THE FOUNDERS OF BRUNSWICK.

"God has so framed our memory, that it is the infirmities of noble souls which chiefly fall into the shadows of the past ; while whatever is fair and excellent in their lives, comes forth from the gloom in ideal beauty."

DR. MARTINEAU.

HAVING traced the history and causes of the separation from the Wesleyan community, we may devote a chapter to a description of some of the characters who took part in it.

Where so many were in agreement, it is impossible to speak of any man as the founder of Brunswick Church and Sunday School. But if any name deserves to be placed first, and to be held in highest remembrance, it is that of JAMES LIVESEY. It was his virtual expulsion from the Wesleyan Society, which caused the smouldering embers of discontent

with the Conference proceedings to burst into flame.
He had been a member of society for half a century,
and was a leader, local preacher, and trustee. His
wisdom and moderation and length of service had
given him a prominent position in the Church. There
are no records which throw any light upon his earlier
life. In business he was a cotton spinner, and ran a
large mill near Bury Bridge, long known as Livesey's
Factory. Livesey Street still perpetuates his name
in the town. His reputation and character were
such, that he was elected President of the second
Annual Assembly of the Wesleyan Association, in
succession to Dr. Warren. For several years he
continued as a leader and local preacher, and in
the latter capacity frequently officiated at the
Tabernacle. During a period of severe commercial
depression. he became involved in business difficulties, and shortly after died, on August 21st,
1842, at the ripe age of 79. His grave may be
seen in Brunswick Cemetery, immediately behind
the old chapel.

JOHN LORD was born at Old Meadows, near

Bacup, of an old Methodist family, in 1783. For
some time he followed the occupation of an excise
officer, but through conscientious scruples he relin-
quished that calling, and commenced business as a
draper in Bury. He was a class leader and local
preacher. His sermons were plain and impressive,
and he had many seals to his ministry. He was
gifted with a talent for music. In his youth he had
been a member of the choir at Bacup, and throughout his life endeavoured to promote the knowledge
and practice of sacred music. So far as his preaching engagements permitted, he fulfilled the duties of
choirmaster in the Tabernacle and in the old chapel,
He joined the Association through a deep conviction
of the righteousness of its aims. In writing an
account of that period, he furnished a clear and
elaborate statement of the reasons by which he was
guided. "My desire is," he said, "that Methodism
may know neither Whig nor Tory, neither Church
and State nor Dissent, but vital Christianity."
John Lord attended the Annual Assembly of 1840,
and his name appears on the Foundation Deed of

the body, which was adopted in that year. The
Rev. T. Hacking sums up his character in one word
—Conscientiousness.

JOSEPH HACKING was a man of substantial position
and high character. He was born near Bury, in
1782. His widowed mother brought up her little
family with great credit and self-denial. She was a
member of the Established Church, and when her
son became converted under the Methodists, she
charged him with undutifulness, and strongly opposed
his associating with such a scandalous set of people,
as she supposed them to be. By degrees her prejudices
subsided, and Joseph became her comfort and support in her declining years. When his mother died,
Joseph found himself in debt. Some of his money
had been invested in looms, and, assisted by a
careful and thrifty wife, he worked hard to get
himself straight. On the very day he got out of debt
his first son was born. He then gave up weaving,
and for a while kept school at a house in Parks's
Yard, but eventually he entered into partnership in
an iron foundry. Afterwards he tried the woollen

business, which proved very unprofitable. He crossed the Atlantic in search of more favourable opportunities; but finding nothing to the purpose, he returned home, and recommenced teaching.

He readily gave himself to Sunday school work, first as teacher, then as secretary, and finally as superintendent, to which office he was appointed year after year. He was also leader of two society classes, in which about forty members were under his care. Being a man of liberal principles, he was fully prepared to support the aims of the Association, though for the sake of peace he would have endured much, rather than disturb the unity of the society. A man of high standing in the Methodist body said that if anyone had left the old Connexion from con-scientious motives, Joseph Hacking was the man. Inobtrusive and diffident in society, he was seen at his best in the family circle. Frankness, candour, and sincerity were his leading characteristics, and his disinterested kindness to strangers was gratefully remembered. He lived but a few months after the disruption, and his funeral sermon was preached in

the old Tabernacle.   His family bears an honoured
name in the annals of Free Methodism.

His son, JOSEPH HACKING, junior, was a man of
mechanical genius, and invented a plaiting machine,
for folding and measuring cloth.   He inherited much
of his father's temperament ; was reserved and
thoughtful, kind and sympathetic.   Though not
physically robust, he was mentally strong, and was
always fervent in his desire to do good.   He never
married, and good-naturedly endured the friendly
banter of his acquaintances on account of his
bachelorhood.   For many years he was a useful and
respected teacher in Brunswick Sunday School, and
there are some who remember how he used to
button-hole young men as they were coming out of
chapel after the evening services, and affectionately
invite them to the prayer-meeting.

Another son of Joseph Hacking, THOMAS, entered
the ministry in 1841.   He became one of our most
able and successful preachers, and occupied the
highest offices in the Connexion, including that of
President.   When our Theological Institute was

established in Manchester, he was appointed First
Tutor, an office which he held for nine years. He
died at Oxford, full of years and honours, in 1893.

Of the remaining children of Joseph Hacking,
ROBERT died when about twenty years of age;
HENRY remained with the Wesleyan body; MARY
became the wife of James Riley (father of Mr. J. H.
Riley); and ELIZABETH was married to Richard
Lord. Mrs. Lord lived to a ripe age. She was full
of kindness and good works, and her cheerful
Christian spirit made her greatly beloved, both in
her family and in the Church.

JOHN ASHWORTH lived in a cottage at Pits o'th'
Moor, where he conducted a small hatting business,
in which a few hands were employed. This industry,
which has developed so amazingly since, was then
among the pursuits which may be termed domestic.
His business necessitated frequent journeys to
Oldham and other markets, where he would carry
his finished "beavers" and other hats, returning with
a fresh supply of raw material. Out of this modest
beginning eventually grew the present concern of

Adam Ashworth and Sons. John Ashworth was an
enthusiastic musician, and for many years trained
the scholars of Clerke Street School to sing at the
anniversaries in Union Street Chapel. If he heard
of a new tune which might be suitable for these
occasions, he would spare no trouble to secure it.
Once he walked as far as Liverpool and back on
such a quest. He is said to have been the first in
Lancashire to teach Sunday school scholars to sing
such elaborate double-choruses as "The horse and
his rider," and "The hailstone chorus." When
Edmund Grundy, of the Wylde, heard that these
were being attempted by such a choir of comparatively untrained voices, he declared that it was
impossible, and offered to give five pounds if they
were successfully rendered. Needless to say, he was
present and fulfilled his pledge.

On one occasion when John Ashworth was
returning from Oldham, with his bundle, he found a
sum of money by the road side. He tried in vain to
discover the owner of it. Money was scarce at home,
and his wife would fain have used it for domestic

purposes. But money was also scarce at the Tabernacle, where they were sadly in want of Bibles for the Sunday school; so John decided that as Providence had placed it in his way it should go to the cause of God.

The families of Hacking, Lord, and Ashworth have contributed not a little to the strength and stability of Brunswick Church, and their descendants are still with us. Many other names are worthy to be chronicled among the originators of this Church. JOHN CLEMISHAW, a faithful class leader and Sunday school worker; RICHARD WILD, a man trusted by employers and friends, and who is said to have had no enemies; HENRY DEARDEN, long known as "blind Henry," who was gifted with remarkable talents, and, notwithstanding his physical affliction, gathered a great store of theological and literary knowledge, and fulfilled the offices of class leader and Sunday school teacher for upwards of forty years; JOSEPH GREEN, a plain, homely local preacher, and a very successful class leader, with a large number of members under his pastoral care;

JOHN RANDLE, a man of independent means, who
owed his worldly position to his conversion through
the Methodists, and devoted his leisure and his gifts
to benevolent work, at the time of his death, in 1842,
holding the office of circuit steward; EDWARD
POTTS, a draper by trade (and father of Mr. Potts,
architect, of Oldham), an acceptable and popular
local preacher, leader of a class which met in his
own house, a kindly visitor of the sick, and also a
circuit steward; DAVID SMITH, a consistent and
godly man, whose descendants played a leading part
in the subsequent history of the Church; JAMES
FISHWICK, a devout class leader, who lived to be over
ninety years of age; JOHN CHADWICK, a useful local
preacher and class leader, who laboured as one that
must give an account; WILLIAM SIDDELL, for many
years a Sunday school teacher and prayer leader,
whose words were few, and were seasoned with
grace; WILLIAM ROBINSON, who lived to be vene-
rated as a patriarch, and whose memory is still fresh
and blessed in the minds of many. ROBERT
BLEASDALE, retiring, and slow of speech, yet who

wielded the silent influence of a holy life more eloquent than words. Richard Buckley, Anthony Cryer, James Barker, Job Holt, William Tuer, Kay Greenhalgh, James Wood, Joseph Kay, James Buckley, Thomas Haslegraves, are also recorded among the early promoters of the work, some of whom afterwards filled positions of responsibility and usefulness.

There are also others, who were young when the secession occurred, and who, in course of time, came to stand in the front rank of workers in the Church and Sunday School. Some of their names will appear again as the story proceeds. It will be enough now just to mention Samuel Smith, Daniel Smith, Isaac Smith, John Fishwick, Joseph Fletcher, Christopher Huddlestone, Charles Atkinson, Samuel Atkinson, Jonas Allen, William Wild, and Edmund Eccles.

These were among the founders and builders of Brunswick, to say nothing of the devout women, who were also their fellow-labourers, who embarked with them upon their enterprise, and shared the anxiety

and the burden.  Few of them possessed much of
this world's wealth ;  but they were strong in faith,
firmly rooted in conviction, and all of them capable
of service.  Secession, the movement may be called,
but schism it clearly was not.  They separated
themselves from the church of their fathers, not
through desire for division, nor love of strife ; but
rather that they might serve God according to the
sanctions of conscience, and free from restraints
which they felt to be irksome, unwarranted, unjust.

## CHAPTER IV.

### THE OLD CHAPEL.

"We have heard with our ears, O God, our fathers have told us, what work thou didst in their days, in the times of old."

*Psalm xliv., 1.*

"O Friends! with whom my feet have trod
The quiet aisles of prayer,
Glad witness to your zeal for God
And love of man I bear."  WHITTIER.

THE old warehouse in Paradise Street is still standing, and consists of three stories, the two first of which were occupied for school purposes, the upper room being used for public worship. Though the place in which the first services of the newly-formed church were conducted was plain and unadorned, and destitute of the architectural and æsthetic accessories which lend a charm of their own to public worship, yet it was so hallowed by the Divine presence, and sanctified by

grace of holy fellowship, as to be appropriately
designated " The Tabernacle." The worshippers
realized the truth of the scripture which says, " The
Most High dwelleth not in temples made with
hands ; " and like the Christians of the first days
who assembled in the " upper room " at Jerusalem,
in the dwelling of some lowly disciple, or in the
river-side oratory, they felt that in the manifest
tokens of Divine favour with which they were
blessed, their humble sanctuary received its truest
consecration.

The tradition of those happy hours spent in
Christian work and worship was long cherished.
The congregations were large, and often crowded ;
the upper room became insufficient, so that it was
found necessary to cut a hole in the floor, that
those below might hear, even if they could not see
the preacher. The ministrations of the Word were
owned of God with many conversions ; the prayer
and fellowship meetings were hearty and demonstra-
tive, as was usual in those days among Methodists ;
and the Sunday school flourished and grew until the

THE "TABERNACLE."

accommodation became too small for the numbers who attended. In the memoir of Joseph Hacking it is said that he often expressed his gratification at the various meetings which were held in the Tabernacle, and remarked that "he believed the old spirit of Methodism and Christian simplicity was getting among them."

The treasurer's book dates back to January, 1836, and the first recorded collection amounted to £23 5s. 6¾d. A "candle collection," made on March 6th, realized £3 14s. 2d. On the other side is a joiners' bill for £25, also accounts for Bibles purchased from Dennis Barker, from January to May, amounting to £4 11s. 5d.

The first sermons on behalf of the new Sunday school were preached on Whit-Sunday, May 22nd, 1836, as the following copy of the circular issued on that occasion will show :—

## WESLEYAN METHODIST ASSOCIATION SUNDAY SCHOOL,

PARADISE STREET, BURY.

On *Whit-Sunday, May 22nd, 1836,*

TWO

# SERMONS

Will be preached in a spacious, substantial, newly-erected
Building, belonging to

MESSRS. WALKER AND LOMAX,

Situate in the angular part of Earl Street and Barlow
Street, the one leading from the New Road, and
the other from Stanley Street,

## BY THE REV. MR. MACKEY,

From Stockport, in the Afternoon; and

## BY THE REV. J. PETERS,

From Manchester, in the Evening.

*A Collection will be made after each Sermon
for the support of the*

SUNDAY SCHOOL.

SERVICE TO COMMENCE AT HALF-PAST TWO O'CLOCK IN
THE AFTERNOON, AND AT SIX IN THE EVENING.

Two hundred & fifty of the Scholars will join in Singing
the Hymns and Choruses,

ACCOMPANIED BY A COMPETENT NUMBER OF

VOCAL & INSTRUMENTAL PERFORMERS.

MR. R. HACKING, LEADER.

SONGS, BY MISS SKINNER, FROM LIVERPOOL.

*Silver will be thankfully received at the Door.*

In the old days in Union Street Chapel, the
"Sermons" was the great eventful day of the year.
"Old John Ashworth" led the singing, many of the
girls were dressed in white, and the collection was
a matter of wonder to those without, and congratu-
lation to those within. Would the traditions of the
past be maintained under the new conditions?
Would the event prove that public sympathy was on
the side of the secessionists? The Tabernacle,
scarcely large enough for ordinary services, was
exchanged for the commodious and unfurnished room
in the factory, which the owners kindly lent for the
occasion, and which was capable of holding 3,000
persons. Two services only, it will be seen, were
held. The orchestra was a large one, and came no
whit behind the old times. John Ashworth had
instructed the "trebles" and "blind Henry" the
"counters," as the soprano and contralto parts were
then named. At the evening service, Handel's "Hallelujah chorus" was sung, and in the middle of the
performance, "Dick" Hacking, the leader of the
instrumentalists, was seen waving his fiddle-bow

enthusiastically round and round above his head, and
when questioned about it afterwards, he said "he
was so excited because it went so well." That
chorus has been sung on many similar occasions
since, and a Brunswick anniversary would scarcely
now be considered complete without it. The afternoon collection amounted to £55 13s. 9¾d., and the
evening to £51 19s. 3¼d.; donations previously
solicited from the Grundys, Walkers, Ashtons, and
Wrigleys of that period, and from many other friends,
amounting in all to £66 9s. 1½d., brought up the
total to £174 2s. 2½d. Great was the rejoicing at
the result of this first public effort, and the friends
regarded it as the harbinger of yet more prosperous
days to come. Among the disbursements required
by the occasion are items for cleaning the windows
and the factory, for music and musicians, and for
beef and mutton, which it is to be supposed were
consumed by the performers and visitors. To
these must be added, a resolution of the school
committee, "That John Ashworth brew three strikes
of malt for the singers."

During the early months of its existence, the Bury society seems to have been unattached to any other, and at the first Annual Assembly, held in Manchester, in August, 1836, it had separate representation, James Livesey and Edward Potts being the appointed delegates. The pulpit during this period was supplied by the several local preachers who were included in the membership, in addition to the assistance which could be readily obtained from Manchester, Rochdale, and the neighbourhood. In the minutes of the preachers' meeting for July we read that Brethren Lee and Thomas Hacking were admitted on full plan, and Brethren Cook, Thornton, and Riley on trial.

In September, 1836, Bury was admitted into the Rochdale Circuit, which was at that time the wealthiest and most influential, and, next to Manchester, the largest circuit in the Connexion. It included also Heywood, and shortly after, Bacup, and comprised, in all, thirty preaching places. The preachers were, of course, obliged to walk the necessary distances to their appointments, and they

frequently conducted three services on the Sunday.
The minister under whose sole pastoral care this
large circuit was placed was the Rev. James Molineux, whose name will appear again at a later stage
of this history.   He was assisted by a staff of more
than forty local preachers, the majority of whom
had been trained in Wesleyan service.   Among these
were several young men who eventually joined the
ranks of the itinerancy;  Edwin Whatmough, Charles
Edwards, and Benjamin Glazebrook.   The following
is a list of the Bury preachers, taken from a " plan "
of 1837.   James Livesey, John Lord, Peter Wood,
John Chadwick, Joseph Green, Thomas Hacking,
Thomas Salter, and Edward Potts, the latter being
" on trial ; "   together with E. W. Buckley, of Bolton.
On a plan dated 1839, there appear the additional
names of James Holt, William Austin, and Thomas
Hawe.

Early in the year 1837, a young man, nearly
twenty years of age, who was a local preacher on the
Bolton Wesleyan plan, having an appointment on a
Sunday morning, midway between Bolton and Bury,

walked forward in the afternoon to the latter place, to visit his friends. To his surprise he found them worshipping in the Tabernacle, instead of in Union Street Chapel. Being urged to preach for them in the evening, he complied, taking as his text " What shall it profit a man?" &c. This was EDMUND WRIGLEY BUCKLEY, a native of Bury, but then residing in Bolton, as an apprentice to the drapery business. He had a taste for reading, which he gratified by making diligent use of the small hours of the morning. His pursuit of knowledge, beyond that required for his calling, displeased his master, who, if he found a book lying about, would not scruple to throw it into the fire or the street. The mind of the young apprentice became stored with useful information, by which he was prepared for his future life-work. His preaching at the Tabernacle that Sunday evening very much annoyed his Bolton friends, among whom he had acquired a considerable popularity. The ministers especially laboured hard to induce him to renounce the Association, going so far as to promise him admission to the Wesleyan

Training Institution.   To this he would not consent,
and, therefore, deemed it best to withdraw.   He was
received on the plan of the Rochdale Association
Circuit, and, a few months later, was recommended
as a candidate for the ministry.

A few weeks previous to the school sermons,
building operations for the chapel in North Street
had commenced.   Like many other similar enterprises
in connection with the Association in Manchester,
Rochdale, Heywood, and other places, it was begun
on the share-holding system.   The subscriptions to
the building fund took the form of shares, upon which
it was hoped that interest would be eventually paid
out of the income from seat-rents and other sources.
There were 1,313½ shares of £1 each taken up on
Brunswick Chapel, and the remainder of the capital
required was borrowed from other sources.

The list of shareholders contains many familiar
names.   James Livesey and his family stood at the
head with a total of 120.   Mr. and Mrs. Thomas
Townend, of Manchester, are credited with 100.
Following these, are John Rawlinson, Bartholomew

Hamer, and Richard Kay, with 30 each; Robert
Hall, James Wood, James Diggle, with 25; James
Fishwick, Joseph Hacking, Edward Potts, Richard
Wild, John Lund, Mrs. Allanson, John Randle,
James Bertwistle, John Petrie, of Rochdale, and
Joseph Wrigley, with 20; and others in smaller
numbers. It was a vain hope to imagine that a place
of worship could ever become a paying concern,
although a dividend of two-and-a-half per cent. was
once actually paid out of the funds of Baillie Street
Chapel, Rochdale. In every instance the system was
speedily abandoned, and the shareholders were invited
to transfer their shares into contributions to the
building funds, which, in the majority of cases, they
willingly did.

The first payment to "spademen and labourers,"
in connction with the new building, appears in April
9th, 1836. Evidently no professional architect was
employed, and the officials seem to have superintended
the erection themselves. The treasurer's book contains a detailed statement of the disbursements as
the work proceeded. Items for lime, sand, stone,

timber, and carting, are interspersed with sums paid for beer, probably supplied as "allowance" for the workmen.

The stone-laying ceremony took place on Whit-Friday, May 27th, 1836. No record of it remains, but there are persons living who can remember being present. The scholars and friends marched in procession through the principal streets of the town, and then proceeded to the ground in North Street. In all probability the actual ceremony was performed by James Livesey, and it is in the recollection of some that he stood upon the stone and addressed the assembly. During the night the stone was removed by some malicious persons, and the articles that had been placed under it were stolen. Since then it has been the custom in Bury, up to a recent date, to place a watch over similar stones until all danger of interference with them was past. The foundation stone of Walmersley Church was laid on the same day, and an account of that ceremony states that the weather was beautifully fine.

THE OLD CHAPEL.

(Now used as a Day School.)

Brunswick Old Chapel, now used as a day school, is plain and unpretentious, the only attempt at architectural adornment being the stone pillars which support the porch. It was entered by a central lobby, over which was placed the choir, and in front of this, stood the pulpit, resting on four wooden pillars. The arrangement of the pews was in the amphitheatre style, and there was sitting accommodation for nearly a thousand persons. The schoolroom was beneath the chapel, and below the street level, but the rapid slope of the land from North Street towards the graveyard, afforded abundance of light. The total cost of the building, and of draining and fencing the land, was £4,000.

The chapel was opened for public worship on Good Friday and Easter Sunday, March 24th and 26th, 1837. The weather was extremely cold, and snow lay thick upon the ground. The preachers were the Rev. Robert Eckett, of London, for many years afterwards the leading statesman of the Association, and Mr. David Rowland, of Liverpool. It is instructive to note the objects to which the

opening collections were devoted. That on the
Friday was on behalf of the Home Mission funds,
and realized £16 4s. 1½d., and that on the Sunday
was in aid of the fund for furnishing the preacher's
house, and amounted to £36 13s. 1d.

# CHAPTER V.

### EARLY PROGRESS.

"The history of the Christian Church has hardly fulfilled the ideal of the New Testament. . . . . But one thing is certain, the Christian character, which came into being among men from the presence of Jesus Christ, has never died out, has never become out of date."

DEAN CHURCH.

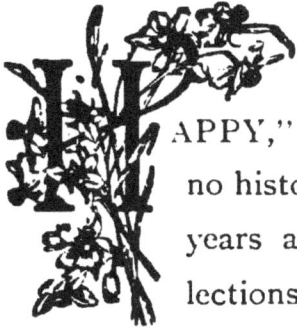

HAPPY," it is said, "is the people that has no history." The records of the next few years are extremely scanty, but the recollections of those days are of spiritual progress and general prosperity. Large congregations assembled on Sundays, numerous conversions followed the preaching of the Gospel, and the class-meetings and lovefeasts were truly means of grace.

The second anniversary of the Sunday school, and the first in the new premises, was held on June 19th, 1837. The preachers were the Revs. Dr. Warren, J. H. Roebuck, and — Aldred, though what

portion of the day each occupied cannot be precisely
determined, and the collections, with some small
donations added, realized £92 17s. 6d. The Rev.
J. H. Roebuck was one of the most brilliant
preachers Free Methodism ever produced. He is
said to have been a prodigy of learning. When but
one-and-twenty years of age, he held a discussion
with the famous secularist, Robert Owen, in Manchester, and acquitted himself with considerable
credit. Unfortunately his career was a brief one,
and in little more than a year after his visit to Bury
he suddenly died.

The Annual Assembly of 1837 was held at Liverpool. The Rochdale and Bury Circuit reported
1,710 members, with 86 on trial. It sent five
representatives, including James Livesey and John
Lord, of Bury. The former was elected President
of the Assembly, which was at once a testimony to
the high estimation in which James Livesey was
held beyond the borders of his own circuit, and an
attestation of the liberal principles on which the
denomination had been founded.

In the *Association Magazine* for August, 1838, there appears a report of the peaceful and prosperous state of the Rochdale Circuit, which had now increased its membership to 2,328. " On the Bury side of the circuit," it states, " the Lord has been graciously reviving His work. Within the last fortnight many souls have been awakened, and not fewer than from forty to fifty have found peace with God." At this time there were three ministers, the Revs. J. Molineux, J. Wolstenholme, and Joseph Handley, the latter of whom resided in Bury. Mr. Handley contributed several memoirs to the magazine, among which is one of Robert, the son of James Livesey, who had lived a worldly life, but who was brought to repentance during his last illness, and led to Christ through the instrumentality of Edward Potts.

At the Assembly of 1840, Bury and the societies associated with it, viz., Heap Bridge, Ramsbottom, Woodhill, and Burrs, were constituted a separate circuit. The minister appointed was Jameson B.

Sheppard, an Irishman, who, at the beginning of the Association, had come over to England and offered his services, which were immediately accepted. He was a man of considerable ability and of fine character, and his affectionate and zealous ministry was warmly appreciated. At the second quarterly meeting of the new circuit, held on December 28th, 1840, Thomas Hacking was recommended to the Connexional Committee as a candidate for the ministry.

Early in 1842, the circuit was extended by the union of a society in Bolton, known as the Wesleyan Refugees, and containing upwards of 250 members. Sheppard visited Bolton, preached on behalf of the Sunday school, and addressed a meeting on the following evening in conjunction with the Rev. John Peters, at which the principles and prospects of the Association were set forth. The amalgamation, however, seems to have been not quite a unanimous one, for in the returns for September, 1843, Bolton is only credited with 150 members, and thirty-two are said to have " gone to the Refugees." From that time until 1847 the circuit was known as the

Bury and Bolton Circuit, the Rev. Robert Rutherford being the first minister on the Bolton side.

The year 1842 was one of great commercial depression, and the collection at the school anniversary fell to the lowest point ever reached, £42 2s. 9d., donations afterwards bringing up the income to £55 10s. 3d.

In December of the same year there is a report of a missionary meeting, the chairman of which was J. Brotherton, the well-known M.P. for Salford. The minister in 1843 was the Rev. David Rutherford, an acceptable preacher, and a man beloved by his ministerial brethren. Two months after his entrance into the circuit, his wife died of typhus fever, in her thirty-second year. Her grave may be seen in the Brunswick Cemetery. Mr. Rutherford was afterwards united in marriage to the sister of the late Joseph Clemishaw.

As illustrating the discipline that was exercised in those days, it is recorded in the minutes that a local preacher was severely rebuked for reading the newspaper on the Sunday; a Sunday school teacher was suspended for frequenting public-houses on the Lord's Day, and another member in high standing was to be seen and spoken to about his having opened his gardens on the Sabbath.

The Assembly of 1844 appointed the Revs. James Molineux and William Middleton as circuit ministers. Middleton remained two years, and was afterwards sent as a missionary to Hamburg. JAMES MOLINEUX was a Lancashire man, and in his early life followed several callings. Beginning as a weaver, he afterwards became a schoolmaster, which was more to his taste. After a time he engaged in business, and had every prospect of worldly advancement, but he abandoned this, and found his true vocation when he entered the ministry of the Wesleyan Methodist Association. He was no stranger to Bury. He had frequently visited the town during his previous term of service in the Rochdale Circuit, and his appointment was as welcome to the people as it was agreeable to himself. He possessed administrative abilities of a high order, and speedily won a prominent position in the denomination. Twice he

was elected President of the Annual Assembly, once
during his ministry in Bury. Thus, for the second
time the Bury Circuit was honoured by the appointment of one of its representatives to the highest
office in the body.

To a richly stored mind, cultured by wide reading,
James Molineux united the gifts of a skilful contro-
versialist. He was a lover of nature. He gazed
with intelligent wonder upon the starry heavens ;
but his favourite study was botany, on which
subject he wrote a popular introduction, entitled
" Botany made easy." His crowning excellence as
a minister lay in his devotion to pastoral work :
to the poor, the sorrowful, and the dying, he was a
welcome visitor. Neat in appearance, cheerful in
bearing, sympathetic in disposition, he was, says
his biographer, " a child among children, and a
philosopher among men." His appointments as a
preacher at the Brunswick School sermons are only
one less than those of John Ashworth, the author
of " Strange Tales."

It would be contrary to history and experience

were this record one of unbroken prosperity. We
sometimes talk of the days of our fathers as if they
were times of unceasing progress and unflagging
spiritual enthusiasm. It is one of the genial infirmities of age to glorify the past. Memory is apt to
dwell longest and most lovingly on its pleasantest
recollections, and conveniently forgets the periods of
depression and decline. It should occasion no surprise, therefore, to hear of such periods in the history
now being told.

No advance was made in the numerical strength
of the circuit during the term of one of the ablest
and most devoted of its earlier ministers. Possibly
the wave of enthusiasm on which the cause had been
launched had now somewhat ebbed. In the lapse
of ten years the freshness would have faded; many
of the first founders had died, and the sense of
responsibility in others had doubtless diminished.
Ten years make many changes in the personnel of a
church, and the losses from various causes are always
numerous. When Molineux began his ministry in
the circuit the aggregate membership was 554, and

JOSEPH HACKING,
Senior.

REV. JAMES MOLINEUX.

REV. E. W. BUCKLEY.

REV. JOHN PETERS.

that of the Brunswick Church 290. In twelve
months the members had fallen to 515 and 276
respectively. These decreases, however, were slowly
recovered, and the number of members fluctuated
until in June, 1847, after three years' labour, it stood
at 556, and was distributed as follows:—Bury 330,
Bolton 161, Ramsbottom 65. This was an experience which would severely test the faith and loyalty
of the members, for though there had been an
increase at Brunswick, yet the circuit as a whole
had barely held its own.

About this time are recorded the deaths of Henry
Dearden, who though denied the blessing of physical
sight, rejoiced in the hope that he should yet see
God's face in righteousness; Mrs. Joshua Lord, the
young sister of Edward Potts; James Wood, who is
described as one in whom conduct and profession
harmonized; John Chadwick, an acceptable and
useful worker; David Smith, a leader, upright, in-
dustrious, and "a credit to the Church;" William
Siddell, trusted by his employers, beloved by his
friends, a prudent and spiritually-minded man.

In the present chapel there is a mural tablet to the memory of Dr. JOHN ALLANSON, who died in February, 1846, at the early age of thirty-one. This young man had been a friend and companion of the Rev. Thomas Hacking. In their youth they had both joined a juvenile class at Union Street, conducted by the Rev. James Roberts, but under the Association Allanson met in the class led by Henry Dearden. He was considered by many as a lad of great promise. In his fifteenth year he began to study for the medical profession. His career was a brief one. He was rapidly rising to eminence, when his intense application to study, and his unwearied diligence in his practice, induced a sickness, which terminated in his unexpected and premature death.

Dr. Allanson is said to have been gifted with considerable poetic taste, and to have written some very creditable verses. The sincerity of his piety is evidenced by the devotional expressions which occur in his private papers, and which were intended for no eyes but his own. He seems to have lapsed somewhat from the fervour of his earlier faith, and in his twenty-first year, he writes, " O, my soul, when shall I be wise ? I here, at this moment, feel it to be my solemn duty to begin afresh to serve the Lord, and to devote myself to Him ; but oh, I raise one obstacle here, and another there, which I fancy is weighty enough to cause me to defer it a little. Nevertheless, I, by the grace of God, if He is with me, and blesses me, am resolved, when I return home, to enter within that threshold, from which I hope never more to depart." As a medical man he was beloved by his patients, to whom, if a fitting opportunity presented itself, he would speak of the concerns of religion.

The story of the erection of the tablet is a revelation of the man. Shortly before his death, he was called in to visit a case of peculiar difficulty. On his return to the surgery he was still utterly at a loss as to the proper medicine to prescribe. He knelt down in prayer to God, and upon rising, instantly prepared a prescription which effected the complete recovery of his patient, who afterwards felt that she owed him her life. When he died, this lady offered the first sovereign if a tablet could be placed in the chapel to perpetuate the young doctor's memory. The inscription on the tablet reads—

SACRED TO THE MEMORY
OF
J O H N   A L L A N S O N ,
OF THIS TOWN, SURGEON,

WHO IN THE VIGOUR OF LIFE, AND IN THE MIDST
OF HIS USEFULNESS, WAS REMOVED FROM EARTH TO HEAVEN.

HE WAS GREATLY BELOVED BY EVERY SECTION OF THE CHRISTIAN CHURCH, REGARDED WITH HIGH ESTEEM BY THE MEMBERS OF THE MEDICAL PROFESSION, AND FAVOURED WITH AN EXTENSIVE PRACTICE, THE PRESSURE OF WHICH PROSTRATED HIS PHYSICAL STRENGTH.

HIS DEATH WAS DEEPLY AND GENERALLY DEPLORED. IN HIM THE EXCELLENCIES OF THE CHRISTIAN SHONE WITH PECULIAR LUSTRE, HIS PIETY WAS SOLID AND UNOSTENTATIOUS, AS A PROFESSIONAL MAN HE WAS AFFECTIONATE, PROMPT, AND ASSIDUOUS, AND IN EVERY DOMESTIC AND SOCIAL RELATION EMINENTLY FAITHFUL.

HE DIED 21ST FEBRUARY, 1846, AGED 31 YEARS.

AS A TRIBUTE TO DEPARTED WORTH, THIS TABLET WAS ERECTED BY THE VOLUNTARY CONTRIBUTIONS OF HIS NUMEROUS FRIENDS.

This is a church, rather than a circuit, history, but a resolution of the March quarterly meeting of

1847 will be of more than local interest. The resolution is, " That Bro. Chew be recommended to the Connexional Committee for home missionary work." The position of a home missionary was at that time the stepping stone to the ranks of the ministry. Richard Chew was then only twenty years of age, but his great abilities soon became apparent, and procured for him admission to the best circuits of the Connexion. His services to the denomination will be set forth in a biography, which is now being prepared by his friend, the Rev. E. Boaden. Richard Chew was twice elected President of the Annual Assembly, and for the last thirty years, he, more than any other man, has moulded and shaped the polity of the United Methodist Free Churches. It is an honour to the Bury Circuit, to have sent forth into the ministry two such men as Thomas Hacking and Richard Chew.

At the close of Mr. Molineux's ministry an additional £10 was voted to him by the quarterly meeting in recognition of his able services in the circuit. He was succeeded by the Rev. W. H.

Walker, who through failing health, afterwards
retired from the itinerancy, and became a cemetery
chaplain, first at Rochdale, and then at Salford.

The next minister was the Rev. Joseph Townend,
a man whose fervour and devotion have earned for
him an honourable place in Free Methodism.  He
came to Bury from Rochdale, after a ministry of
unqualified success.  In his autobiography he says:
"We met with a kind reception from this modest,
unpretending, but intelligent people; with whom I
lived and laboured, with great pleasure and some
profit, for eighteen months, and I was sorry that we
had to be so soon separated."  Joseph Townend
was an evangelical preacher of the old school, and
shrank not from declaring the sterner aspects of
Christian teaching.  His message was delivered
with great power; the chapel was frequently crowded,
and many were awakened to repentance.  He was
also a very zealous temperance advocate, and
frequently lectured and preached on the subject.  A
famous sermon of his on Belshazzar's Feast, in which
he depicted with fearful effect the evils of indulgence

in strong drink, is still remembered. His favourite designation of the public house was "drunkery."

The cause of the separation from Bury, to which he refers, was a request from the Connexional Committee that he should proceed to Australia as pioneer missionary of our Churches in that colony. That committee met for the first time, in Bury, in November, 1850. There is an interesting account of the occasion in the pages of the *Wesleyan Methodist Association Magazine*. The Rev. Robert Eckett preached on the Sunday. A missionary meeting, on the Monday, is said to have been the best ever held since the establishment of the Association in Bury. John Kipling, of Darlington, was in the chair, and the speakers comprised many of the connexional leaders of that day. On Wednesday, the Rev. Robert Eckett gave a lecture, on the origin, constitution, and discipline of the body, when John Petrie, of Rochdale, the Connexional Treasurer, presided; on the Thursday a temperance meeting was held, with Joseph Townend in the chair. Joseph Townend acceded to the request of the committee,

to the great grief of the circuit : his last Sunday
being the Brunswick School anniversary, when the
chapel was filled to overflowing.  His autobiography
furnishes a detailed narrative of his perils and
triumphs as a missionary, at a time when life in the
colonies was of a much more primitive character
than it is to-day.

The interim between Townend's departure for
Australia, and the Assembly of 1851, was filled up
by the Rev. E. W. Buckley, who, after a brief
itinerant career of thirteen years, had returned to
Bury broken down in health.  Edmund Buckley had
literally worn himself out by his earnest devotion to
the work he loved.  His record is one of unceasing
toil and of almost uninterrupted success.  His diary
frequently tells of crowded congregations and
numerous conversions.  One entry, when stationed
in the Ruabon circuit, says, " Since Sunday morning
I have preached nine times, walked forty-two miles,
and ridden seventeen.  But," he adds later, " no
toil, no labour, can possibly be too much, when the
salvation of souls is our object."  Preaching was

never easy to him, and sometimes his earnestness
carried him beyond his strength. Twice he was
compelled to seek rest through physical exhaustion,
and at last was obliged to relinquish the work. He
settled in Bury, with his wife, who was the daughter
of James Fishwick. Though not fully restored to
health, he consented, after a brief holiday in Lincoln-
shire, to undertake the superintendency of the
circuit until the Annual Assembly.

The account of his closing days is extremely
pathetic. The Rev. John Wesley Gilchrist was then
the superintendent minister, but Edmund Buckley
occasionally officiated. He preached his last sermon
in Brunswick Chapel in December, 1851, when he
announced that he would, God willing, preach to the
young on that day three weeks, should his health
permit. Man proposes, but God disposes. In the
commencement of 1852, he said to a friend, " It is
my appointment on Sunday next at Brunswick
Chapel, but I am not able to fill it, and probably
never shall preach again; well! the Lord's will be
done,—I bless God that I have employed my little

F

talent in His service—praise the Lord for my early
conversion." His death occurred shortly after, in
the thirty-sixth year of his age. His widow is still
living, and a member of our Church, though probably
a stranger to most of the present generation. She
has proved, through forty-four years of widowhood,
the truth of her husband's dying words to her, " I
am going home, but God will take care of you."

Some lines were written in the *Magazine*, to his
memory, from which we quote,—

"O why so early lay him with the dead?
Ardent, hopeful, when he spoke of Christ,
Impassioned, eloquent, his whole soul athirst
For souls.   .   .   .
No other theme he knew—no other Saviour sung;
This, to this alone, in life, in death, he clung."

John Lord died on January 3rd, 1852. In the
later period of his life, Providence had smiled upon
him, and he had attained to a creditable position in
the world. He was a man of sound judgment,
which was frequently brought to bear on Church
affairs. The seriousness of his disposition was
brightened by a sense of humour, and he was
essentially a man of peace. His life had not been

without its sorrows. He had had business trials of
more than ordinary difficulty. His household had
been broken by death, two daughters having died
only a few years previously. The eldest of these,
Rachel, died of consumption in 1850. She had
been an earnest Sunday-school teacher, a collector
for the missionary and dorcas societies, the chief
joy of her life being to serve Christ in His
Church. In the midst of her weakness she said, " I
never could have thought that I could be so happy."
Mrs. Lord, who was the daughter of William Kay,
of Woolfold, had at one time seemed likely to be
taken away by death, but she was spared to survive
her husband.

Towards the close of his life John Lord's
spiritual experience ripened, and his delight in
Christian service increased. He was deeply attached
to the cause in the origin and progress of which he
had had so considerable a share. He seemed to
have an intuition that the end was near, and at
the last lovefeast he attended, he said, " There is
nothing, next to my own soul's welfare, that I care

more for than our society; O! that the Lord would raise up faithful servants." He then mentioned by name some of his old fellow-labourers, and expressed the hope of soon joining them in heaven. The end came with startling suddenness, his sufferings only lasting about half-an-hour, but his death was full of triumph. His youngest brother, the Rev. William Lord, Wesleyan Minister, was at that time governor of Woodhouse Grove School, and his three sons, Richard, William, and John Kay Lord have, in varied capacities, been spared to serve the Church.

The Sunday school anniversary of 1852 was a memorable one, from another cause than that it was the farewell of Joseph Townend. It was also clouded over by a melancholy occurrence on the following day. William Burgoine, a young Sunday school worker, and a trustee of the chapel, was accidently killed while repairing a water-wheel at Radcliffe. He was only twenty-five years of age, and had taken a prominent part in the festivities of the previous day. His death created a profound sensation throughout the town, and evoked much sympathy from all classes of people.

# CHAPTER VI.

## EARLY PROGRESS (CONTINUED).

"If it be the happiness and glory of a bishop to live in a devout spirit, full of holy tempers, doing everything as unto God, it is as much the glory and happiness of all men and women, whether young or old, to live in the same spirit."

WILLIAM LAW: *Serious Call.*

AT the Annual Assembly of 1852, the Rev. JOHN MATHER was located as minister of the Bury Circuit. Happily, Mr. Mather is still with us, the oldest surviving minister of Brunswick Chapel, living in the enjoyment of a ripe and vigorous old age. Though he has retired from regular circuit work, he has not ceased to render active service. For several years he has been pastor of the church at Parkhills; occasionally he officiates at Brunswick and other chapels in the neighbourhood, besides being in request as a special preacher in various parts of the

country.   Throughout his life, Mr. Mather has been
a successful man.   His itinerancy is a remarkable
record.   Entering the ministry in 1844, he has
laboured in some of the best circuits of the denomination, in each of which he has remained never less,
and often longer, than three years.   He has filled
the office of President of the Annual Assembly, and
has frequently had a seat on the Connexional
Committee.

When he first came to Bury, he was in the
strength and fulness of his young manhood.   He
had already earned a considerable reputation as a
preacher.   Possessed of a fine musical voice, he
could use it with splendid effect.   When he was
fairly warmed to his work, his words flowed freely
forth in eloquent periods, until the fire that glowed in
his soul communicated its warmth to the congregation, and moved them to earnest and sympathetic
response.   In method, he skilfully combined the
expository with the practical, and few preachers
have excelled Mr. Mather in his elucidation of the
teaching of St. Paul.   He was deeply, rather than

REV. JOHN MATHER.

widely, read. The Bible was, and is, his text book, and Jesus Christ his central theme, his favourite topic being the Gospel as a revelation of God's love to man, calling forth man's love to God, and man's love to his brother. Blessed with a strong constitution, he has scarcely known what weariness meant, and at times, perhaps, has seemed impatient with the weakness of others. He has falsified the prediction of some Wesleyan friends who, hearing him preach on one occasion at Ramsbottom, said, " If he goes on preaching like that, he won't live long."

Mr. Mather has been an excellent pastor, and in Bury, as in all his circuits, has won much regard through his visitations. He never stood on ceremony, but dwelt among his people as one of them, and claimed to move in and out as a guide, a reprover, and a father. He was discreet in his administration of circuit affairs. Previous to his coming, there had been some difference of opinion between the minister and the officials, which had led to the former's withdrawal of his acceptance of a

second year's invitation.   It is characteristic of Mr.
Mather that, at his reception service, he begged the
friends not to mention the matter in his presence,
and, consequently, in a short space of time, it was
buried and forgotten.

Mr. Mather's first ministry in Bury was not
marked by any very striking events, but progress
was made in every department of Church work, and
the membership steadily increased.   There were
several notable revivals of Christian work, during
which many young men who have since played a
leading part in the history of the place, were
converted to God, and under Mr. Mather's
direction were trained up in ways of Christian
usefulness.   Mr. Henry Brown, the oldest local
preacher on the present plan, preached his trial
sermon on March 21st, 1853.   Mr. John Stockdale
was received as a preacher on trial on June 13th in
the same year.   In the March quarter of 1855, the
names of Joseph Meadowcroft and Mr. John Ashton
appear as on trial, while Messrs. Joseph Bickerstaffe
and Lambert Fletcher are to have their names

marked by initials, and to receive appointments with a view to their becoming preachers.

In the summer of 1852 the chapel was beautified, and some structural alterations were made, under the superintendence of Joseph Clemishaw and Daniel Smith, the re-opening services being conducted by Mr. Mather on September 5th.

An alteration was also made in the legal settlement of the property. The plot of land upon which the premises are built, had been taken on a system of leasehold which was at that time common in this locality, and the disadvantages of which must have frequently created anxiety in the minds of the lessees. The lease was conditional on the duration of three lives, and on an annual rental of £56. The lives in this case were not particularly good, and what with the heavy ground rent, the interest of the chapel debt, and the cost of an insurance policy upon the youngest of the three lives, the trustees were considerably hampered in financial matters.

The lessee's interest was ultimately purchased for £650, and the lease being surrendered to the Earl of

Derby, the father of the present Earl, his lordship, to his great credit, granted a new one for 999 years, at a rental of £30 per annum, whereupon the trustees displayed their fidelity to the denomination of which they formed a part, by settling the premises upon the Connexional Model Deed.

At the request of the March quarterly meeting, in 1853, Mr. Mather wrote an account of the prosperity of the circuit for the *Wesleyan Methodist Association Magazine.* In that report he refers with evident pleasure to the spiritual successes which had been granted to them, and says that "the circuit is in perfect peace." In addition to the prosperity at Brunswick, preaching was commenced at Radcliffe, in a room at the Lyceum, which was rented at half-a-crown a week, and steps were also taken towards the erection of a suitable place of worship at Limefield.

At the close of Mr. Mather's ministry a resolution was unanimously passed by the circuit meeting, thanking him for "his zealous and faithful labours during the past three years," and expressing its gratitude to God "for the peace and prosperity" which the churches had enjoyed for that period. Reference was also made by the brethren assembled, to the services rendered by Mrs. Mather, and to the esteem in which she was held by the people.

It may be well, now, to pause in our narrative in order to note a few of the characters who were connected with the Church at that time.

One of the special objects of Mr. Mather's pastoral care, was Alice, the wife of Anthony Cryer. Her maiden name was Horrox, and her family was well known in Heywood. She was born near Edgworth, in 1796, and from her childhood had been associated with the Methodists. She was a woman of exceptional character, and an ardent and consistent Christian. Up to middle life she had enjoyed the best of health, when cancer made its appearance, and it became necessary that she should undergo a surgical operation. Just before the operation was performed, she asked of a relative present, "Is it not said, ' He giveth power to the faint ' ? "

" Yes ! " it was replied, "' and to them that have no might, He increaseth strength.' "

" That will do," she said, and with the courage of one relying upon Divine help she yielded herself into the hands of the surgeons. She afterwards frequently said, that the day was as happy a one as she had ever enjoyed.

The operation was perfectly successful, but another enemy speedily attacked her, in the shape of rheumatism, which compelled her to keep her bed for the remainder of her days. She bore her pain with fortitude, and enlivened the long and tedious hours by reading twice through the New Testament.

Among the visitors who sometimes called upon her, was the Rector of Bury, the Rev. E. J. G. Hornby. It was the rector's practice upon entering, to say, in the words of the Apostolic benediction, " Peace be to this house!" to which Mrs. Cryer always devoutly responded, "Amen!"

One day he said to her, " I am surprised, Mrs. Cryer, that a woman of your common-sense should go to a Methodist conventicle."

" Sir," she replied, "under God I owe all that I know and enjoy in this world to the Methodists.

In my young days I never went to school; I had to work early and late, and I learnt to read by following the hymns and the reading of the scriptures in the Methodist chapel; it was there, too, that I found the way of salvation."

"That is all right," said he, "but the men who preach there have no right to teach."

"But, Mr. Hornby," she continued, "the Catholics say that *you* have no right to teach."

The rector was puzzled for a moment, and then he said, "To make it plain to you, Mrs. Cryer, the Catholic Church was like a man who had got his face blacked, and we Protestants have washed it!"

"And," she quickly retorted, "we Methodists thought it wanted a little more, and we had another try!"

This may not have been conclusive reasoning on either side, but it displayed the ready wit of the humble Methodist, and her steadfast adherence to conviction, and it exhibited the rector hoist with his own petard.

Mrs. Cryer soon died a happy and triumphant death. Her husband said to her, " I think you are getting into the valley."

" Yes ! " she replied, employing a reminiscence of the " Dairyman's Daughter," a book which she had read and loved ; " Yes ! but it is not dark ! "

Another house which the ministers of those days used to frequent, was that of the Misses Ashworth, at Pits o'th' Moor. Maria and Rachel Ashworth were the daughters of John, and sisters of the late Adam Ashworth, of Walmersley Road. Their house was a preacher's refuge. It was likened to the house at Bethany, " not wholly in the busy world, nor quite beyond it," where Lazarus and his sisters dwelt; but here there was no Lazarus, only Martha and Mary. Miss Rachel was the " Martha " of the cottage, whose pride was in the whiteness of the hearth, and the shining brightness of the pans. Miss Maria was the " Mary," the saint of the household. She was a devout and holy woman, of a type that is now extremely rare ; precise and strict in her habits, and frequent in prayer, for which exercise she had set times in the day, with which nothing was allowed to interfere. When the hour arrived, she would leave the little shop, by which the two sisters added to their livelihood, and retire to her room, where she would kneel beside a chair, and pour out her soul to God. That chair is still treasured as a sacred heirloom by the family. One night, the roof of the house being somewhat out of repair, the rain percolated through, and some drops fell upon her neck; she continued her devotions notwithstanding, and afterwards said, " Neither rain nor devil shall hinder me at my prayers."

Her joyful heart expressed itself in song, and if no customer was in the shop, she would be nearly always singing. Her favourite hymn was that noble one of Charles Wesley,

"Come, O Thou Traveller unknown,"

which so capable a judge as Archbishop Trench considered to be about the finest hymn in the English language.

The sisters were true friends to the preachers,

whom they recognised and welcomed as servants of
God. Many were the gifts which their kindness
prompted them to send, for the preachers were not
very liberally remunerated in those days. Nothing
gave these ladies greater pleasure than to provide a
meal for the preachers, or to lodge them for the
night if they came from a distance. It was never a
question with the officials of the church as to who
should entertain the minister, for one house was
always open.

For thirty years a society class assembled weekly
in their house, under various leaders. Among those
who attended this meeting was Peter Scowcroft. In
his early life he had been fond of worldly sports and
pastimes, and had lived regardless of religion, but
now that he had been converted, his chief pleasure
was found in the means of grace. Peter was a man in
whom quaintness and true spirituality were strikingly
blended. Sometimes he would say that he was
"like a cork, for when he was persecuted he always
came out at the top." He was a godly and consistent man, but his simple piety seems at times to

.have exposed him to the scoffs of his fellow workmen. It is related that when one of his persecutors had suddenly died, Peter came to the band meeting on the following Saturday, and when the opportunity arrived for him to relate his experience, he began by saying, in the most solemn tones, " They are dead that sought the young child's life ! " He was in the habit of responding aloud during public worship. This was somewhat disagreeable to the more decorous among the congregation, who remonstrated with him, but Peter replied, " If th' cork doesn't fly, th' bottle 'll brast ! "

Peter and John Standring were bosom friends and comrades in Christian work. They were known as " Peter and John," and might frequently be seen together, visiting the sick, or assisting the preachers at the prayer meetings, after the public services, on Sunday evenings. On one of these occasions, when the Rev. John Adcock was conducting the prayer meeting at Limefield, Peter engaged in prayer. In the course of his utterance he quoted the words of Scripture, " Let me die the death of the righteous,

G

and let my last end be like his." Kneeling near to
him was Abraham H——, who responded, " Aye,
Paul were a good mon !" Peter paused in his
prayer, and turning to him, solemnly corrected him,
saying, " It wern't Paul, Abra'm, it were Balaam !"
and then proceeded as before.

Class meetings at that time were most regularly
attended. To be absent from class for any length of
time without sufficient reason, was to run serious
risk of dismissal. The meetings, moreover, were
well sustained. Every person present felt it a
duty to take some part, and an inclination to keep
silence was regarded as a temptation of the devil.
Class meetings were held in the higher and lower
vestries at the chapel, but other classes assembled in
private houses. In addition to the one just referred
to at Pits o'th' Moor, there were meetings at
Foundry Street, Freetown, Crostons, Gigg, Heap
Bridge, Limefield ; also at the houses of Edward
Potts, Anthony Cryer, Mrs. Randle, Mrs. Lord,
Mrs. Hacking, and other friends. The lovefeasts
were held quarterly, and were nearly always crowded;

the passport was the quarterly ticket of membership, without which none were admitted, and the minister usually sat in the vestry ready to supply these if they were required. The band meeting, on the Saturday evening, was also a popular means of grace, and was regarded as a preparation for the Lord's Day.

Is it to our credit to have to write of these meetings in the past tense? They are not indeed extinct, but they exist chiefly as survivals of the past. True, the life remains, though it may manifest itself under different forms. Each generation must needs express its religious emotions in ways that are most natural to it. Still the Christian life demands fellowship; the communion of saints is absolutely essential to spiritual health and growth, and if the Christianity of to-day is ever to display the force and fervour which characterized that of our fathers, it will only do so through the stimulus of the exercises of united prayer and praise, and by the more frequent interchange of holy thought.

Mr. Mather's successor, in 1855, was the Rev. JOHN PETERS, an Irishman by birth, and possessed

of the best qualities which are associated with the
Celtic race. He was quick, bright, impulsive, and
witty; but these were balanced by the more sober
virtues, and no man was more methodical, reliable,
punctual, and attentive to all his engagements and
duties. A brilliant preacher and an admirable platform orator, he was in frequent requisition for pulpits
outside his own denomination, and as an advocate of
various public institutions. He had had the advantage
of a good education, being intended by his father for
the ministry of a Presbyterian body in Ireland. His
mind revolted, however, from the Calvinism in which
he had been trained, and he associated himself with
the Wesleyans, who, in Ireland, were then a despised
and persecuted people. But John Peters was a lover
of ecclesiastical liberty, and Conference Methodism
was too narrow and exclusive for him; so he threw
in his lot with the reformers of his day. At
considerable pecuniary sacrifice he accepted the
invitation of the newly formed Wesleyan Methodist
Association, and came over to England to devote

his energies to that cause. From this decision he never swerved.

For many years he occupied a high position in the Connexion, being twice elected to the office of President. Few men can adequately fill so large a sphere, and it is indicative of his exceptional powers that, while Peters was popular abroad, and a leader in Connexional affairs, he could also faithfully discharge the duties of a circuit minister, and win the love and esteem of the people he lived to serve.

He took an active interest in the education of the young, and did much to encourage the formation of mutual improvement classes for the benefit of the Sunday school teachers and young men of his con-gregations. The Brunswick Mutual Improvement Society owes its origin to him. The subjects discussed were mainly Biblical and theological, and his wide knowledge and keen intelligence were employed in the elucidation of the most difficult and perplexing themes. At the close of his ministry in Bury, which lasted only two years, the members of the improvement society presented him with a set

of Barnes's "Notes on the New Testament," together with an address, which expressed regret at
his removal, and gratitude for the care and fidelity
he had displayed as president of the society.

In December, 1855, occurred an important event
in the history of the Church,—the opening of the
first organ in Brunswick Chapel. From the time of
the secession, the singing had been accompanied by
stringed instruments of various kinds. An amateur
orchestra is not, as a rule, the most admirable from
an artistic point of view, and stringed instruments
in the hands of unskilful players do not discourse
the most delightful music. The service of praise in
Brunswick Old Chapel, while it was hearty and
sincere, was not, in those days, quite beyond
criticism, and the time arrived when the trustees
and leaders jointly agreed to purchase an organ. It
was not a new instrument, but it was an excellent
one for its purpose. It underwent several enlargements and was afterwards removed into the new
chapel, where it remained until the erection of the
magnificent organ which now occupies its place. It

was built by Bolton, of Liverpool, and contained twenty musical_stops. The committee appointed to carry out the work, and to obtain subscriptions, consisted of Joseph Hacking, junior, Daniel Smith, Richard Lord, Peter Ormerod, William Wild, and Samuel Smith. The choir gallery was lowered to provide for its reception, the pulpit brought forward, and two new entrances were made into the chapel.

The opening sermons were preached by the Revs. John Peters and John Mather, Mr. Mather being then stationed in Rochdale. As a sequel to these proceedings, and as marking the transition from the old order to the new, the following resolutions were passed at a subsequent trustees' meeting : " That the Limefield trustees be offered the lesser bass fiddle for the sum of twenty shillings." " That the Heap Bridge trustees be offered the double-bass fiddle for the sum of thirty shillings."

During these years the congregation at Brunswick was favoured by occasional visits from the popular preachers of the denomination. The Rev. John Guttridge, the orator of Free Methodism, was then

at the height of his fame.    Few men could command
such crowds, or could sway them so effectually as
he.    Cultured people might criticise his methods,
but the common people heard him gladly, and he
was a strong force for good in the churches.    For
three years he was stationed at Heywood, between
which place and Bury there were quarterly inter-
changes.    He preached the school sermons in 1852,
and took part in a series of successful revival
services in 1853.    He afterwards frequently came to
Bury to preach and lecture, and was always sure
of a large and receptive audience.

In the year 1856, the Rev. Marmaduke Miller
paid his first visit to Bury.    If Guttridge may be
said to have been the orator of the denomination,
Marmaduke Miller may justly be designated its greatest teacher.    It is vain to compare one preacher with
another ; as the Apostle says, "all have not the
same gifts."    Perhaps at no time was Miller ever
so popular or could attract such numbers as
Guttridge.    His excellence lay in other directions,
and as a moral and spiritual force perhaps no man

has exercised so deep and permanent an influence on the thought of the churches.

This first visit was at the instance of the Brunswick Temperance Society, then a vigorous and powerful organization. A deputation of young men, including Mr. John Ashworth, Mr. Ben Fish, now of Bridgeport, America, and the late Henry Moorhouse, waited upon him in his lodgings in Manchester. Miller was then in the prime of manhood, his reputation rapidly rising. "Well, gentlemen, what is your business?" he asked. If the young men were taken aback by the dignity of his manner, they were still more astounded at the occupation in which they found him engaged. He was sitting with slippered feet resting upon the mantel-shelf, reading Shakespeare !

If we have learnt, in our day, to appreciate the rich treasures of our English literature, and to claim all that is good and true and nobly beautiful in art and science for Christ, it is in some degree owing to the influence of such men as Miller, who have been courageous enough to look beyond the bounds

of a narrow theology, and strong enough to speak
and act upon the truth they have seen.

The deputation succeeded in their errand. Miller
came to Bury and lectured on "Luther and Loyola,
a comparison and a contrast." The lecture was a
very fine one, delivered with much of the dramatic
force which the lecturer exerted less frequently in
his later life, but which he then wielded with admirable effect. It is still remembered how vividly he
described the incident of Luther throwing his ink-
stand at the devil, suiting the action to the word,
until the audience looked to see the ink-splash on the
chapel walls. That was the first of many visits, and
until his death, in 1889, Marmaduke Miller was
always welcome at Brunswick.

# CHAPTER VII.

## "LET US RISE AND BUILD."

"The glory of this latter house shall be greater than of the former."
*Hag. ii.*, 9.

"Therefore, when we build, let us think that we build for ever. . . . And let us think, as we lay stone on stone, that a time is to come when those stones will be held sacred because our hands have touched them, and that men will say as they look upon the labour and wrought substance of them, 'See! this our fathers did for us.'"

RUSKIN : *Seven Lamps.*

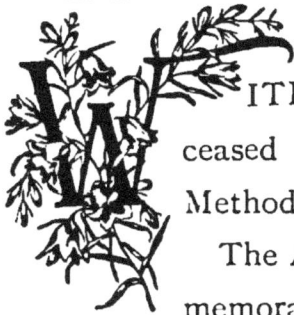

WITH the year 1857 Brunswick Church ceased to bear the name of "Wesleyan Methodist Association."

The Annual Assembly of that year was a memorable one. It met at Rochdale, and was signalised by the amalgamation of two branches of the Methodist family,—the Association and the Wesleyan Reformers. A new designation became necessary, and that of " United Methodist Free Churches" was adopted. The Bury Circuit cordially approved of the union, and accepted the new name which was its sign and seal. The union has proved to be one of unqualified benefit to all the parties concerned, and the distinction between Associationists and Reformers was speedily obliterated in unity of life and organisation.

The minister appointed to Bury in that year was the Rev. Edwin Wright, who remained in the circuit three years. He was admired as an able and effective preacher, and as a man of remarkable kindness and generosity of heart. His wife was the sister of Mrs. Marmaduke Miller, and held a warm place in the affections of the people.

In the trustees' minutes of July, 1857, there is a resolution to the effect that a sum of £20 be paid annually to the circuit stewards towards the maintenance of a home missionary, part of whose duty it should be to officiate at interments. This led to the engagement of Mr. William Stott, who seems, however, to have been employed in a more general way to co-operate with the minister, than other missionaries have been in subsequent times. Mr.

Stott was a protégé of the Rev. John Mather. He
came from Halifax to Rochdale, where he was
employed as a mechanic at the works of Mr. John
Petrie, during Mr. Mather's ministry in that circuit.
Mr. Mather interested himself in the young man,
and encouraged him to consecrate his gifts to the
service of Christ. He had him frequently at his
house in the evenings, where he directed him as to
his reading. In course of time he came on the plan
as a local preacher, in which capacity he achieved
great success as a winner of souls. It was at Mr.
Mather's recommendation that he came to Bury.
He sacrificed a good situation, against the wishes of
his father, and became the first Brunswick missionary, at a salary of a pound per week.

"At that time," writes Mr. Stott, "things were in
a poor way, financially, numerically, and spiritually.
It was in the month of September that I entered
Bury; that good and true friend, Richard Lord, met
me at the railway station and conducted me to my
lodgings in North Street. All my material belong-
ings were contained in a large carpet-bag, which,

upon entering the room, I threw upon the floor. We both went down on our knees, and I felt constrained to pray this prayer, ' O Lord, souls or glory in twelve months ! souls or glory in twelve months ! ' And Mr. Lord, in his quiet way, prayed, ' Lord, give this young man souls for his ministry, but spare his life also.' Those prayers were answered in crowded congregations and many conversions."

One Sunday night the heat was so intense that Mr. Stott felt obliged to take off his coat before commencing to preach. A Sunday or two later, he had the misfortune to send off a glass globe from the gaslight, which flew in a thousand pieces, and created a sensation. The incident became widely known, and proved a capital advertisement, for on the following Sunday hundreds were unable to get into the chapel.

Mr. Stott did not claim to be a preacher in the intellectual sense, but he was all on fire with evangelistic zeal. He was, moreover, a man of prayer, and seemed to fulfil the description given in the Acts of the Apostles, "full of faith and of the

Holy Ghost." On one occasion, while he was preaching at Brunswick, some of the leaders gathered in the vestry for prayer, and it was said that the power of God was sensibly felt during the service. After service in the chapels, he would hold meetings in the old theatre, on the fair ground, or some other public place, and seemed never to tire of proclaiming the gospel of salvation. His example was contagious. The Church was stirred as it had never been before, and not only was the chapel crowded on Sundays, but all the meetings for Christian fellowship on the week-nights were full and enthusiastic.

Between Mr. Stott and his superintendent there was never so much as a suspicion of jealousy. Mr. Wright rejoiced in the prosperity of the work of God, and the young man occupied the pulpit at Brunswick almost as frequently as he. All the places in the circuit shared in the revival, particularly Heap Bridge and Ramsbottom. "At the latter place," says Mr. Stott, "a large band of young men were won to Christ, and we used, when

I was planned there, to meet in summer days at five o'clock in the morning, in an old quarry some distance out, and the earnest prayers and hallowed praises of those young men were a prelude to richer blessing."

To the spiritual success of those days was mainly due the movement which culminated in the building of the new chapel. At one of the anniversary tea meetings Mr. Stott promised the first five pounds. He says, " My promise came like an inspiration, and was at once followed with noble sums from families such as the Smiths, the Ashworths, the Lords, the Hackings, the Fletchers, the Isherwoods, the Ormerods, and many others, so that in a few weeks over one thousand pounds were forthcoming to form a building fund."

Mr. Stott left the circuit after two years of earnest and arduous labour. He was recommended by the quarterly meeting as a suitable candidate for the ministry, but having adopted Baptist views, he ultimately joined that denomination, in which he has had an honourable and successful career. At first pastor of a church at St. John's Wood, London, of which he may be said to have been the founder, he was afterwards invited to assist the late C. H. Spurgeon, at the Metropolitan Tabernacle. He now holds a pastorate at West Norwood.

The movement towards a new chapel passed through several stages. At first it was proposed to erect day schools, but that idea was soon abandoned in favour of a proposal to enlarge the old chapel. That again was found to be inadequate, whereupon Mr. Samuel Smith introduced a plan for a new chapel in the amphitheatre style to seat twelve hundred persons. Architects were invited to prepare pencil sketches, and it was agreed to spend not more than £3,000. One of these sketches was adopted, and though nothing further was done for several months, the resolutions passed by the trustees show how fondly they clung to the arrangement and style of the old place.

Then a fresh development occurred. The trustees heard of a chapel, which had recently been erected in Hanover Street, Sheffield, and a deputation,

H

consisting of Robert Isherwood, Daniel Smith,
Joseph Hacking, John Fishwick, and William Wild,
was appointed to visit and report upon it. The plans
of that building were obtained, and it was finally
resolved to carry out the proposed chapel on the
same dimensions, and in the same external style as
that at Sheffield; internally, the friends thought
they had improved upon their model. Mr. Chatt-
wood, architect, of Bury, was entrusted to make the
neccessary drawings, and to superintend the work.

The Rev. Joseph Kendall came to the circuit in
1860. He belonged to a family of preachers. His
father was a Primitive Methodist, and, of ten sons,
six were received into the Christian ministry.
Joseph Kendall was a studious man, and strove hard
to be a good minister of Jesus Christ. His sermons
were composed with elaborate care, and delivered
with fervour. If he had a weakness, it was in
pastoral work, where his natural reserve and shy-
ness in the company of strangers, caused him
sometimes to be misunderstood. A second minister
was appointed, for the first time since the division

from Bolton, and Mr. Kendall had for his colleague for one year, a young man named Joseph Walker, who was much beloved, and who subsequently went to Australia.

The preparations for the new chapel were now proceeding apace. More than £2,000 had already been promised, and this was to be supplemented by a bazaar. It was the first time that an effort of this kind had been employed at Brunswick, and the record of it is therefore interesting on that account. It is a question whether this method is the most suitable for raising funds for religious purposes, and we can imagine the heart-searching which the proposal must have occasioned among some of the older members of the Church. True, such an effort diverts energies which ought to be employed in other and more spiritual ways, but over against this may be set the enlistment of energies that would be otherwise unemployed; and the sacrifices which are made of time and money, the spirit of unity in aim and effort that is called forth, together with the success with which such an enterprise is generally

crowned, may possibly counterbalance all imagined
disadvantages.   I cannot pretend, however, to solve
such a difficult problem, and, as a matter of fact,
the problem has solved itself: bazaars are and will
be held.

The Athenæum was engaged, and the bazaar
opened on Wednesday, May 8th, 1861.   The
circular announcing it was an extremely plain and
modest production.   No elaborate art was employed
in the decoration of the stalls, nor any captivating
programme of entertainments offered to add to the
attractiveness of the bazaar.   The only effort in
this latter direction was an announcement that there
would be "performances on the pianoforte by Mr.
Spragg."   The opening ceremony was in striking
contrast to the long drawn out proceedings on such
occasions at the present day.   The Rev. J. Kendall
announced two verses of the time-honoured hymn,
"Praise ye the Lord," &c.   Mr. Thomas Holt, as
chairman of the committee, made a short speech,
in which he paid a tribute to the ladies, and to
gentlemen like Messrs. John Fishwick, John Stock-

dale, and Robert Isherwood, for the services they had rendered, and then the business commenced. The newspaper reporter states that he was "completely nonplussed" in his efforts to take the stock of the whole affair. There were ten stalls, a post office, a weighing machine, a chair which had belonged to the grandfather of Sir Robert Peel, all of which were used as expedients for adding to the funds. On one stall was a chair, of which the cabinet work had been done by a teacher, and the embroidered needlework with which it was adorned, by a scholar in the school. This was purchased for £7, and presented, together with a quilt, to Mr. David Smith, in recognition of his services as organist for more than five years. The bazaar was open for four days, and the total amount realized, less expenses, was £672 10s. 6½d.

The work of building the new chapel commenced immediately. The basement story, comprising the present schoolroom, was undertaken upon a contract of £880. Twelve months elapsed before the corner stone of the chapel was laid, and this corner stone represented, in fact, the first stone of the chapel walls.

The ceremony took place on Whit-Thursday, June 14th, 1862. The trustees could have made no better choice than when they entrusted this duty to Samuel Smith. He was not only the largest donor to the building fund, but he had been associated with the Church from its commencement, and had been treasurer since the formation of the Trust. No man was more highly respected. As a successful man of business, and as one of the town's Commissioners, he held a foremost place in public life. But his chief interest was centred in Brunswick; on its behalf he had made many sacrifices, and his best life was bound up with its success.

Large preparations had been made for the ceremonial, a procession of nearly two thousand persons paraded the town, including contingents from Limefield, Heap Bridge, Elton, and Ramsbottom, and a vast concourse of people assembled on the ground. Unfortunately the heavens were unpropitious, and a steady downpour of rain shortened the proceedings. The trowel presented to Mr. Smith was the gift of Mr. Joseph Downham. After the stone was "well and truly laid, in the name of the Father, the Son, and the Holy Ghost," three cheers were given, and, amidst the pouring rain, Handel's "Hallelujah chorus" was sung. The company then adjourned to the chapel, which became so crowded that the children had to be sent into the school. The meeting was addressed by the Revs. S. S. Barton, President of the Annual Assembly, and J. S. Withington. In the evening there was a great tea-meeting. Mr. Smith presided, and speeches were made by the Revs. Marmaduke Miller, John Peters, Edwin Wright, William Stott, H. M. Cuttell, J. Walker, and J. Kendall, and by Messrs. John Stockdale, Joseph Hacking, Richard Lord, and Robert Hall. The choir sang "The heavens are telling," "Worthy is the Lamb," and the "Hallelujah chorus." Miss Lomax sang "I know that my Redeemer liveth," and the Misses Green and Winward the duet, "O lovely peace."

These details may not be of much interest to the

reader who is a stranger to Brunswick; but it is possible they may be a means of perpetuating the memory of some notable names in its history, and of calling up recollections in many minds of what must have been a red-letter day in their lives.

In January, 1863, further tenders were accepted for the completion of the chapel; the erection, apparently to many, proceeded too slowly, but, as the work progressed, and the structure rose in its imposing proportions, it became an object of admiration throughout the neighbourhood. The photograph will represent its appearance and style, far better than any verbal description of its architecture. The chapel, from floor to ceiling, is forty feet high, it is one hundred feet long, and seventy-five feet wide. The height of the school-room underneath is eighteen feet. The total cost was £7,250.

The building was opened for Divine worship on Wednesday, December 7th, 1864. Again the weather was inclement, but there were very large congregations. The new Bible and hymn-book used

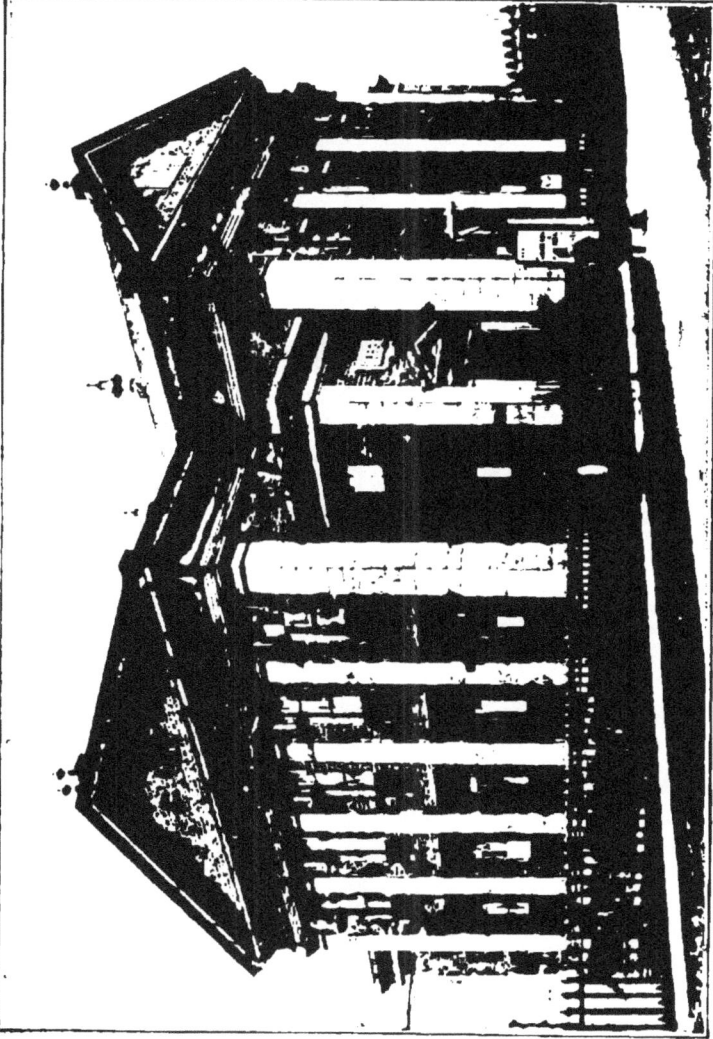

THE PRESENT CHAPEL.

in the pulpit were presented by James Fishwick and his daughter Mrs. Buckley. The clock in front of the gallery was the gift of Mr. Nelson. The dedicatory services commenced with the " Hallelujah chorus," Master Edwin Smith presiding at the organ. The Rev. W. R. Brown conducted the devotional exercises, and read the lesson. The preacher in the afternoon was the eminent Congregationalist, the Rev. Enoch Mellor, M.A., of Liverpool. His sermon was based on Acts iii., 1—8, and was one of his finest efforts, original, chaste in diction, and massive in argument. The Rev. Marmaduke Miller officiated at the evening service, his text being from Haggai ii., 2—4. The sermon was intensely practical, and marked by the simple, short, and yet powerful sentences, which characterized his style; though it was said that Miller was frequently heard to better advantage than on that occasion.

The opening services were continued for several weeks, and the preachers were the Revs. J. S. Withington, Jos. Colman (President), Dr. Stacey (New Connexion), John Guttridge, William Stott,

E. Walker (Wesleyan), W. Roseman (Independent), and Mr. John Ashworth, of Rochdale. The total amount collected at these services was £563. It was the general opinion that never before, in the town of Bury, were services so numerously attended nor so triumphantly successful.

When it is remembered that the chapel was erected and opened during the trying season of the cotton famine, this success is all the more striking. Notwithstanding the marvellous generosity of the friends towards their Church, they were also able to spare enough to contribute handsomely to the funds that were raised on behalf of the distressed factory operatives.

INTERIOR OF THE CHAPEL.

## CHAPTER VIII.

### THE NEW CHAPEL.

---

"The blessed work of helping the world forward, happily does not wait to be done by perfect men; and I should imagine neither Luther nor John Bunyan, for example, would have satisfied the modern demand for an ideal hero, who believes nothing but what is true, feels nothing but what is exalted, and does nothing but what is graceful."

GEORGE ELIOT.

---

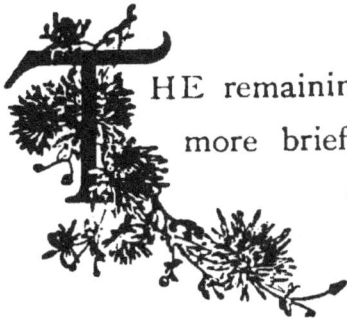

THE remaining portion of this history may be more briefly told. The events which it comprises are well within living memory, and most of the ministers who have laboured in the circuit since the opening of the new chapel are still engaged in active service. This, however, cannot be said of those who were actually in charge while the building was in progress; of Joseph Kendall and H. M. Cuttell, who were present when the stone was

laid, and of W. R. Brown, who was superintendent
when the chapel was opened.

The Rev. Henry Martin Cuttell had his first
sphere of ministerial labour in Bury, and entered
upon his work with youthful enthusiasm, but his
promising career was cut short by death, in the
twenty-ninth year of his age.

The Rev. William Roberts Brown was a Cornish-
man, and one of the earliest ministers of the
Association, having entered the ministry in 1835.
As a preacher he was not brilliant, but plain, pointed,
and earnest. " He was characterised," says Marmaduke Miller, " by strong, round-about common
sense," somewhat reticent, but deeply devout, and
entirely sincere. During his ministry in Bury he
was elected President of the Annual Assembly. He
died in 1885 at Christchurch, in New Zealand, where
he had gone on a visit to his youngest son, who was
head master of the Grammar School there. Mr.
Brown's colleagues were the Rev. Joseph Shaw, now
a congregational minister, and the Rev. John T.
Hodge, who is still engaged in the ministry of our

churches, and to whom is due the credit of having cleared off the debt from Ramsbottom old chapel.

On December 29th, 1865, the venerable William Robinson died, at the ripe age of seventy-seven, leaving behind him the blessed memory of a saintly life. He was one of those characters who are remarkable, not so much for what they have done, as for what they have been. There is little to tell of the outward events of his life, but all who knew him, speak of the wonderful charm of his personality. His family was deeply and tenderly attached to him and to the members of the Church, he was a brother beloved. When the secession took place, although his sympathies were with the movement, he seems to have hesitated at taking the final step which would sever him from the Wesleyan body, but Joseph Hacking said to him, " Come thou with us, and we will do thee good," and he at once threw in his lot with the seceders. He was a devoted labourer in

the Sunday school, and, at the time of his decease, was leader of two society classes, and a trustee of the chapel. As his was the first death that had occurred among the trustees since the opening of the new chapel, it was arranged that the burial service should be read in that building; and it was made a rule, that for the future, a like privilege should be within the right of the family of any trustee, under similar circumstances.

The Rev. Charles Ogden came as superintendent minister in 1866, and in 1867 he was joined by the Rev. Ormerod Greenwood. Mr. Ogden's sermons were extremely interesting, and Mr. Greenwood's ministry was not without its fruits. Each of these ministers has had an honourable record, and they are both greatly beloved in all the circuits where they have laboured. Mr. Richard Heyworth was also employed in circuit work at this time, and was so popular as a preacher, that the quarterly meeting recommended him as a candidate for the itinerant ministry. He, however, joined the Baptists, among whom he has laboured for many years in Rossendale.

The Rev. Edward Browning succeeded Mr. Ogden in 1868. He was more than forty years of age when he offered himself as a candidate for the work of the ministry; nevertheless he became a powerful exponent of the Gospel; his discourses were of a highly rhetorical character, and were intensely theological. He died in 1875. The junior minister was the Rev. Samuel Sellars, whose genial disposition gained him many friends.

During this period the chapel was beautified, and an effort made to reduce the debt. At a breakfast-meeting held on Good Friday, in 1869, so much enthusiasm was manifested that, in the space of ten minutes, £300 was promised towards these objects. The re-opening services took place on Thursday, October 14th, the Rev. J. A. Macfadyen, of Manchester, being the preacher; and on the Sunday following, the pulpit was occupied by the Revs. George Warne and Joseph Townend.

On September 28th, 1869, Brunswick Church suffered an immense loss in the death of SAMUEL SMITH. Mr. Smith was born in 1810, of Wesleyan parents, and joined the society when eighteen years of age. His business career commenced with a situation under Mr. Bartholomew Hamer, in whose service his father was also employed. He speedily won the confidence and esteem of his master, eventually married his daughter, and was admitted to a share in the partnership. As a business man he was known for his integrity, punctuality, and diligence, and speedily merited a considerable degree of success. He was not, however, a man to be spoilt by prosperity, but continued to maintain the same simple and unostentatious habits in social life as heretofore. He was accustomed to read the Bible daily with his family, and no matter how weary he might be, the exercises of family worship were never omitted.

It was said, "Samuel had three topics, Shares, Cotton, and Brunswick Chapel." For forty years he was a Sunday school teacher and superintendent.

Among the other offices he filled were those of leader, trustee, treasurer of the Trust, treasurer and financial secretary to the Sunday school, and president of the temperance society. In each of these positions he displayed the same earnestness and fidelity which characterised his business life. He has been found at nine o'clock on the Sunday morning, singing the opening hymn in his class-room alone, because the time had come, and not one of his members was present to join in the devotions.

Ministers of the circuit, and other friends who knew him well, testify of his moral uprightness and consistent godliness. He was never known to yield to anger, and when provoked would quietly turn away. His generosity knew no bounds; not only did he contribute liberally to the funds of the church and school, but his purse was ever open to relieve the necessitous and the suffering. And all this was done in a simple and unostentatious manner, often privately, and, as it were, by stealth. He was a cheerful giver, and the poor and the fatherless

I

blessed him. He also found a sphere for his activity in public life, serving for nine years as one of the town's Commissioners. He had, it is said, his angularities, but taking him all in all, he was one of the grandest men in the long roll of the worthies of Brunswick Church, which owes not a little of its strength and stability to the impress of his powerful individuality.

A marble tablet in the chapel bears this inscription :—

IN MEMORY OF

M R. SAMUEL SMITH, OF BURY.

A FAITHFUL HUSBAND AND AFFECTIONATE FATHER ;

A DILIGENT AND UPRIGHT MAN OF BUSINESS ;

AN EFFICIENT SUNDAY SCHOOL TEACHER ;

A DEVOTED CLASS LEADER ;

AN EXEMPLARY CHRISTIAN ;

WHO HAVING SERVED HIS GENERATION BY THE WILL OF GOD,

FELL ASLEEP IN JESUS, SEPTEMBER 28, 1869,

AGED 59 YEARS.

THIS TABLET WAS ERECTED BY HIS FELLOW-TEACHERS
AND FRIENDS IN CONNECTION WITH BRUNSWICK SABBATH SCHOOL.

Some in-memoriam verses were written by Mrs. E. C. A. Allen, in which the following lines occur :—

"A good man and true hath departed
  From the world—from the Church, from his home;
And many a heart-stricken mourner
  To weep o'er his grave-bed shall come.
The young, whom his wisdom hath guided;
  The needy, whom he hath supplied;
The brother and neighbour, who found him
  A friend, sympathising and tried;

    .   .   .   .   .   .   .

Let us copy his goodness and virtue;
  Let his Saviour and Lord be *our* Friend;
Then we soon shall rejoin the departed
  In the glory that never shall end."

At their first meeting after the death of Mr. Smith, the trustees elected his son, Mr. Samuel Smith, as their treasurer, and that office has been held by a Samuel Smith from the commencement unto the present time.

The Assembly of 1870 marks the advent of the Rev. W. R. SUNMAN, one of the ablest and most popular ministers ever appointed to Brunswick. Mr. Sunman was, and still is, a man of indomitable energy and unbounded capacity for work. His preaching power was of a high order, and in the

days to which we now refer, he was accustomed to
set forth the evangelical beliefs which he firmly
held, with a vehemence, a rhetorical and dramatic
skill, which were then much admired.

Owing to the unsatisfactory state of the circuit
financially, it had been determined to work it for
that year with only one itinerant minister, the
labours of the Ramsbottom preacher (the Rev. H.
T. Chapman) being confined to that town. Mr.
Sunman entered upon his formidable task with
an enthusiasm which at once commanded success.
His zeal became contagious. Some of the older
men, the founders of the Church, and the builders
of the new sanctuary, were still living and able
to render service ; such men as Robert Bleasdale,
Daniel and Isaac Smith, Richard Lord, John Stockdale, Peter Scowcroft, James Ashworth, and others ;
and besides these there was quite a host of
young men who have, in course of time, become
the leaders and officers of the Church. So hearty
was the co-operation between the minister and the
people, that the cause quickly rallied, the congrega-

REV. W. R. SUNMAN,
PRESIDENT OF THE ANNUAL ASSEMBLY, 1895.

tions increased, many were added to the Church, and funds were raised for furnishing a second minister's house, and to pay both ministers what were then considered good salaries. Various expedients, it is true, had to be employed to raise money, for a very large sum was required each year in order to meet the interest on the chapel debt. The offertory system was inaugurated, and the "service of song," then a novelty, was first introduced. One Sunday evening the "Pilgrim's Progress" was given with musical accompaniments; the chapel was crowded, and the collection came to £26. On a succeeding Sunday afternoon the service was repeated, when £15 was realized. Special thanks were voted for this effort to Mr. Jesse Meadowcroft, the choir, and the young people who had assisted them.

Mr. Sunman also conducted Sunday evening services for children. These were of an evangelistic character and were extraordinarily successful, securing the decision of large numbers of young people for Christ, and leading to the formation of several junior society classes.

But Mr. Sunman's labours were not confined to
the pulpit. The *Bury Monthly Visitor* was started,
under his editorship, as the organ of Brunswick
Church; five thousand copies were distributed gratis,
and the *Visitor* soon became a power in the town.
He also organised, during the four years he was in
the circuit, an old people's tea and treat at
Christmas time, and in this he was freely supported
by the generous contributions of friends. Outside
the Church, he commenced a series of Sunday afternoon lectures to working men, which were given in
the Athenæum, and which became extremely
popular. His opening lecture on "Saturday night
in Bury" made a sensation. In it he depicted the
scenes he had witnessed while perambulating the
streets of the town, in disguise, until a very late
hour. The lecture was mainly designed to expose
the evils of drunkenness, and to enforce the value
and necessity of temperance.

Politically Mr. Sunman was a force, and few
speakers were so welcome on the Liberal platform.
His experiences during the election of 1874 may

be best decribed in his own words. "To the Liberal party in the country it was disastrous, but we managed to return the old Liberal member, Mr. R. N. Philips, by a substantial majority. I well remember the stir of that time, and took my full share of the work. I was at the old warehouse in Paradise Street when the floor fell in and killed nine people, and I stood with Mr. Philips and a few others, in the horrible darkness, on that portion of the floor which was supported on a wall, and which therefore did not give way. But I shall never forget the terrors of that occasion."

The extent of Mr. Sunman's influence may be estimated from the fact that on his removal from Bury he was publicly presented with a purse of one hundred guineas, together with other substantial gifts, subscribed to not only by members of the Church, but by political and other friends who admired his work. To this day few former ministers are more warmly welcomed than Mr. Sunman, and the news of his election as President of the Assembly of 1895, was very gratifying to many Bury friends.

In the year 1871, Ramsbottom was constituted a separate circuit, and Mr. Sunman was joined at Bury by the Rev. Thomas Ashcroft, who was also a man of more than average ability, richly endowed with popular gifts, and possessed with an ambition to become a useful minister of Jesus Christ. Mr. Ashcroft was well received in the circuit, and soon became celebrated both as an able preacher and popular lecturer. His sermons are highly spoken of, and his ministry was fruitful in conversions. Both these ministers were men of strong individuality,—young, enterprising, and aggressive. It is well-known that during a portion of that time there were differences of opinion, and that matters did not run quite smoothly in the circuit. Doubtless the blame did not lie wholly with the ministers, and both proved themselves sufficiently strong in the sympathies of the members to break, for the first time, the tenacious Methodistic rule of a three years' itinerancy, and to secure an invitation to continue their labours for four successive years.

No more suitable choice of a successor to Mr. Sunman could have been made than that of the Rev. John Adcock. Eminently peace-loving and conciliatory, unassuming and reticent, he was yet a man of intense conviction and faithful to principle. He was deeply sympathetic, rejoicing with those that rejoiced, and weeping with those who wept, fulfilling the prophet's characterisation of a good man, "a hiding-place from the wind, and a covert from the tempest."

Mr. Adcock was also a pulpit orator of the first order. The pulpit was his throne. The following description of his preaching abilities, from a character sketch in the *Methodist Monthly*, is at once graceful, eloquent, and just :—

"A superb voice under splendid control; a faultless deliverery, with its piano and forte passages, its crescendos and diminuendos, all carefully appointed as in some classic oratorio ; a passionately poetical temperament, never losing itself in wild rhapsody nor mixing its figures in confusion, but sustaining itself gracefully in flights where others would

wildly gyrate ; evangelical to a fault, and sometimes so
simple that he ran the risk of being counted childish—such
was Mr. Adcock in his golden pulpit days.  We never
heard him grapple with any of the great metaphysical
difficulties of the day ; but we have heard him describe
heaven's new song until our ears seemed to catch the
distant refrain of the redeemed.  We never heard him
address himself to the scientific difficulties besetting many
thoughtful minds, but we have heard him speak of home,
and, while hearkening, found ourselves carried back to the
dear old family hearth, and to our boyish days, the past
rushing back upon us, with its far-off innocence and ex-
tinguished aspirations.  Epigram also, as well as description,
enters largely into Mr. Adcock's preaching, and he can
frame an anecdote as few of his fellows can."

No event of striking moment occurred during Mr.
Adcock's ministry, but the membership rose to the
highest point it has reached for the last thirty years.
It was with profound sorrow that the friends heard
of his intention to leave them at the close of his
second year.  Somebody had evidently blundered,
or Mr. Adcock had not rightly understood the feeling
of the circuit towards him.  Extraordinary efforts
were made to induce him to reverse his decision, but

it was too late, for he was already engaged to the Hanover Circuit, Sheffield.

His subsequent career has been a distinguished one. When he came to Bury he had just laid aside the office of President, and since he left he has occupied, for six years, the arduous post of General Missionary Secretary. On relinquishing that office he laboured for another six years in one of the Manchester circuits, and is now living in comparative retirement in that city, bearing in his old age the memories of a noble and useful life, the modest recipient of the gratitude and affection of those whom his ministry has blessed.

The Rev. Henry Holgate joined Mr. Adcock in 1875, and remained during the two years' ministry of the Rev. R. D. Maud. The former is still a successful minister of our churches, and the latter, after giving full proof of his abilities, has " fallen on sleep," and is remembered as an earnest and faithful preacher, a true friend, and a man of deep and genuine piety.

In September, 1876, Mr. John Stockdale resigned

the office of circuit secretary, which he had held for sixteen years, and went to reside at Southport. He had formerly been a local preacher among the Wesleyans, but during the ministry of Mr. Mather he transferred his services to Brunswick, and from that time became intimately associated with every branch of Church work. He was for many years a teacher of the young men's class in the Sunday school. Frequent reports of the progress of the circuit, from his pen, were sent to the Connexional magazines, and to him the writer of this history is indebted for some valuable suggestions.

The first suspicion of a ritualistic spirit seems to have made its appearance in the Church about the year 1877, in the expression, on the part of the trustees, of a desire to intone the " Amen " at the close of each service. The matter was discussed at a congregational meeting called for the purpose, and previous to which Mr. Maud had preached a sermon from the text, " And let all the people say Amen." He was accused at the meeting of having delivered a " political sermon ; " the resolution was, however, carried, but it was never carried out in consequence of the dislike to it which was manifested by a few of the older members. Since the introduction of the new chapel hymn book we now sing "Amen" after many hymns, but the prayers of the minister on behalf of the congregation are still offered without audible response on their part.

The Revs. Arthur Hands and Philip Bennett were the ministers appointed in 1878. Mr. Hands had just been elected Corresponding Secretary to the Annual Assembly, an office which he held for three out of the four years of his residence in Bury; and upon leaving the circuit, in 1882, he was elevated to the Presidency. During this period the congregations at Brunswick were large, and the membership was well sustained. True there was the chronic difficulty of maintaining the circuit funds, but by means of sales of work and other efforts, debts were speedily removed.

In the month of April, 1879, the alarming discovery was made that the chapel roof was giving way. The first indications were observed on the morning of the school anniversary, and upon examination it was found that the centre of the ceiling had sunk out of level to the depth of eleven inches. The anxiety of those who were acquainted with this fact may be imagined, and right glad they were when the day closed without a catastrophe. The trustees were promptly called together to grapple with the difficulty. Mr. John Burgoine, the secretary, was requested immediately to secure the inspection of the premises by an architect. The situation was pronounced dangerous in the extreme ; the chapel was closed, and steps were taken to repair the mischief. At first it was thought that the whole of the roof would have to be removed, but it was eventually determined to raise it by means of screw-jacks. It was then properly secured and effectually strengthened, and in the end was declared to be safe enough to "drive a locomotive and train across."

All this necessitated the beautifying of the chapel, and the total cost incurred was £1,226. No lamentation was made over it, but trustees and congregation set about the work with vigour and liberality, and when the chapel was re-opened by the late Dr. Macfadyen, its beauty excited universal admiration.

While the chapel was closed for these repairs, two young men were summoned to Bury to preach trial sermons, with a view to their entering upon the Connexional ministry. Mr. Hands being a member of the Connexional Committee, was appointed to hear them, and to conduct them to Manchester on the following day for their theological examination. The service was held in the old mortuary chapel, which was inconveniently crowded, and the two youths fulfilled their trying task with diffidence and fear, one of them little dreaming that in a few years time he would be pastor of that very Church, and that it would be given to him to write these chronicles.

One personal reference emboldens the writer to crave indulgence for another. He would acknowledge his indebtedness for something of his training as a local preacher and his preparation as a candidate for the ministry, to the late Rev. Charles

Bentley, who was at that time stationed in the Macclesfield circuit.

Charles Bentley proceeded, after a happy and fruitful ministry, from Macclesfield to Bury, in 1881, as successor to the Rev. P. Bennett. His early career gave promise of great usefulness. Possessed of a powerful voice, and somewhat declamatory in style, he was a striking preacher; frequently choosing out-of-the-way texts, and striving to present the truths of the Gospel in a fresh and attractive manner. He was a diligent and prayerful student, a conscientious pastor, a true and sympathetic friend, and a successful fisher of men. Though morally and intellectually strong, his bodily presence, like that of St. Paul, was weak, and he had been little more than a year in Bury before his health hopelessly broke down. A voyage to Australia was undertaken by medical advice, but it proved of no avail, and he returned home only to die at his father's house in Bradford, on March 3rd, 1884, in his thirty-fifth year.

In the year 1881, Robert Hall, a member and trustee of Brunswick Church, was appointed Mayor of the Borough. The Mayor invited the members of the Corporation to accompany him to his usual place of worship, and a considerable number accepted the invitation. They came with due pomp and ceremony, attended by the police, the fire brigade, and other officials of the town. The Rev. Arthur Hands preached from Acts x., 38, " Who went about doing good," and in the course of his sermon made fitting reference to the presence of the Mayor and Corporation in the congregation.

In December of the same year, ROBERT BLEAS-DALE died. He was of Quaker extraction, a fine-looking man, and as good as fine-looking. He had a kindly soul overflowing with love to all, and his life was rich in good works. His generosity was ungrudging and unostenta-tious. Like William Robinson, his greatness lay in his goodness. In business and

K

other meetings he spoke little, but his very presence
carried an influence which was powerful for good.
He was a model Sunday school teacher, never absent
and never late ; happy in teaching the young, and
most affectionate in his appeals. Beloved by every-
body, he was an especial favourite with children.   In
his old age he spent a considerable part of his time
about the chapel and school : sometimes entering the
day school, standing by and watching the children
at their work; sometimes chatting with the chapel-
keeper about the old days, or wandering in the
cemetery, and reading the inscriptions upon the
graves of his departed friends and dear ones.

One day the little daughter of a member of the
congregation was missing from home, and her friends
made a long and anxious search for her. They
discovered at last that she had been in the graveyard,
where she had gone, as she said, to look for her
baby brother, who lay buried there. She said that
she had seen Jesus, and had been talking to Him.
At first this was a great mystery, and was set down
to her childish imagination, but it was afterwards

discovered that he whom she thought was Jesus, was
Robert Bleasdale, whose white hair and genial face
and gentle manners had seemed to her to embody
all that she had heard and thought of the Saviour.
Truly Robert Bleasdale adorned the doctrine of
God, his Saviour, and men took knowledge of him
that he had been with Jesus.

ISAAC SMITH died in August, 1882. He was the
youngest of the three sons of David Smith. Like
his brother Samuel, Isaac joined
the Wesleyan society in his
young manhood, and became a
member of Joseph Green's
class. He afterwards joined
the class led by James Fishwick, whom he eventually
succeeded as leader. In this sphere of labour he
excelled. Punctual and regular in his attendance,
he was also kindly and fervent in spirit, and strove
to make the meetings interesting and profitable.
When twenty-four years of age he commenced to
preach the Gospel, passing his examination for

full plan under the Rev. James Molineux.  He was
also employed in Sunday school work for many
years, and occupied, at various times, most of the
offices in connection with that institution.   In 1861
he received a present from the young men's class
of a family Bible and a large hymn book, in
recognition of his labours.

For some time he was in the habit of inviting a
number of young men to his house on Sunday
mornings for prayer.  On other occasions he would
meet them at the chapel, at seven o'clock, where one
of them would in turn be encouraged to preach.
Isaac was not sparing in his criticisms, and if the
young novice chanced to wander from his subject,
he would be quickly called back to the point, or if he
showed a disposition to extend his remarks unduly,
would be pulled up with the words, "Always give
over when you have finished."

In his business relations religion was the domina-
ting power in his actions, and by his uprightness and
consistency he gained the respect of his fellow men.
He was married, in 1846, to Sarah, daughter of

William Siddell, who still survives him. His home
life was of the happiest description, and family worship was conducted with unfailing regularity. He
was blessed in his death. In the hour of extremest
weakness his spirit seemed to manifest its greatest
strength. When one of his family asked him,
" Could he still trust in Jesus? " " Yes," he
answered, " I can trust him with all my heart."

One of his last sayings was " It will do; " upon
which Mrs. Allen wrote some lines, including the
following :—

> " ' It will do,' are the words upspringing
>    From a confidence deep and sure ;
> ' My heart in its trust is singing,
>    His mercy shall ever endure ;
> It has been no cunning fable
>    I believed and sought to teach,
> The grace of God is able
>    My dying need to reach.' "

# CHAPTER IX.

## RECENT TIMES.

"When our names are blotted out, and our place knows us no
more, the energy of each social service will remain."

JOHN MORLEY.

BY a singular coincidence, the Rev. Joseph
Kendall was stationed in the circuit during
the holding of the two great bazaars,—the
one in 1861 on behalf of the building fund
of the new chapel, and the other in 1882 for the
removal of the chapel debt. The resolution of the
writer to narrate briefly the events of recent years,
may surely be relaxed for the purpose of describing
this magnificent effort.

Mr. Kendall's second appointment to Bury commenced a few months before this bazaar was held.
We must go back, however, more than twelve

months for the origin of it. To the young men of
the first Bible class is due the honour of its
initiation. At a trustees' meeting held on March
11th, 1881, a letter was read from the above class,
signed by Mr. Andrew Buckley, secretary, and containing the following resolution, which had been
proposed in the class by Mr. James Holt, and is
well worthy of being put on record : " That in order
to induce the trustees to take action in the direction
of liquidating the chapel debt, this class guarantees
to furnish a stall for a general bazaar for that
object." The debt then stood at £3,654.

The trustees promptly and gratefully responded to
the challenge thrown down by the young men, and
agreed that a sum of not less than £2,000 should be
aimed at. The congregation was immediately called
together to drink tea at the expense of the trustees.
They gave their hearty and unanimous agreement to
the proposal for a bazaar, and appointed an executive
committee, with Messrs. William Stockdale, J. H.
Riley, and John Downham, secretaries; Mr. S.

Smith, treasurer; the Rev. A. Hands, president; and William Wild, vice-president.

A subscription list opened among the trustees secured promises to the extent of £500, the Sunday school undertook to raise a like amount, and the branch churches were also invited to co-operate. Collecting books and cards were issued, sewing meetings organised, various devices employed, and for the next eighteen months, men, women, and children were busily engaged in promoting, by every lawful means, this great enterprise; and, wonderful to relate, though all energies seemed to be turned into this channel, the several organisations of the Church did not appreciably suffer, nor were the school anniversary collections in any wise diminished.

Philips Hall, the largest and most suitable room in the town, was engaged, and a "grand Oriental bazaar" was opened there on October 18th, 1882. The Rev. J. Kendall presided, Mr. J. H. (then Councillor) Riley, presented the report. There was a great gathering, including, amongst other notabilities, the Mayors of Bury and Rochdale. The

opening address was given by Mr. Robert Leake,
M.P., in the absence, through illness, of the Member
for the Borough (R. N. Philips, Esq.), and it was a
highly finished and suitable oration.

The Brunswick Church and congregation furnished three of the stalls, the Sunday school two, and
the branch churches two. The stalls were decorated
with mottoes and ornamentations of an eastern
character by Mr. F. W. Livesey (a grandson of James
Livesey) and Mr. James Shaw, from designs supplied
by Mr. Sam Smith. The bazaar remained open for
ten days, and realized in subscriptions and sales the
noble sum of £3,300.

Another tea-drinking took place to celebrate the
success attained, when votes of thanks were enthusiastically passed to all the workers, and congratu-
latory speeches made in honour of the result, which
had been arrived at with perfect good feeling and
unanimity.

The ungrudging toil, the cheerful generosity of
the members and friends of Brunswick Church on
that occasion, deserve to be recorded. Never,

before or since, has such a triumphant effort been made on behalf of any religious or benevolent institution in the town of Bury, and, perhaps, the achievement is unsurpassed in the annals of any other church in the denomination. It did not quite extinguish the debt, but it came very near to it, and had it not been that alterations were subsequently made, which cost nearly £1,600, the remainder of the debt would naturally have quickly disappeared.

But it is impossible for an organisation which is alive and enterprising, to stand still and rest upon its laurels ; and early in the following year the day school was internally reconstructed, and a new mortuary chapel erected in the cemetery, which, together with the balance remaining, created a new debt of £1,950.

The Rev. S. W. Hopkins became junior minister in 1883, in succession to the lamented Charles Bentley. Joseph Kendall removed in 1885, and was followed by the Rev. T. W. Townend, nephew of Joseph Townend, the memory of whose ministry in the years 1849-50 was so affectionately cherished.

Mr. Townend's sermons were brimful of instruction, logical in arrangement, and forcefully delivered. In his administration of circuit affairs he displayed great wisdom and discretion. An important piece of legislation was completed in November, 1885, in the signing of the new Trust Deed, by which the premises were vested in a strong body of trustees, whose names are representative of the leading families associated with the Church. This result was not achieved without difficulty and anxious thought, and special mention is made of the services rendered in connection with it by the Revs. J. Kendall, T. W. Townend, Edward Boaden (Connexional Chapel Secretary), and Mr. Richard Lord.

In the year 1886 Brunswick Church attained its Jubilee. This highly interesting event was celebrated on Good Friday, April 23rd. Few persons, if any, were then living who had played a prominent part in the circumstances commemorated on this occasion, but there were many who carried youthful recollections of the beginnings of the society, and who had been scholars in the old "Tabernacle" school.

The celebration commenced with a reception in the day school, and the promoters were gratified to see the large numbers of old friends who presented themselves from all parts of the kingdom. After the hand-shaking was over, addresses of welcome were delivered by Messrs. L. Fletcher and John Smith, and the Rev. John Mather. In the afternoon there was a social gathering, in which many old scholars and teachers took part. The proceedings terminated with a great meeting in the chapel. The Rev. T. W. Townend presided, and paid a fitting tribute to the past history of the Church. Mr. Lambert Fletcher next read a concise historical sketch (afterwards printed and widely circulated), in which mention was made of many of the facts which are given with fuller detail in this book. Testimony was then borne by various speakers to the value of the instruction they had received, and the benefits they had derived from this institution. The Rev. Thomas Naylor related how he had come to Bury, in 1873, as assistant to Messrs. Driffield, that he owed his conversion to the preaching of the Rev. T. Ashcroft, and had become a member of Isaac Smith's class, and been employed as a teacher in the Sunday school, until his removal to Sheffield. Mr. John Cryer, of Rochdale, blessed God for the ministrations of the Rev. Joseph Wolstenholme, and looked back with gratitude to the love-feasts and other means of grace which he had attended here in days past. Mr. George Ormerod, of Southport, said that he had occupied most of the offices in con-nection with the Church and school. Messrs. J. Meadowcroft, C. Talbot, Jas. Holt, and others also spoke, and the Rev. S. W. Hopkins appealed to the young, reminding them that the future of the Church depended very much upon what they were determined to make it.

This is the briefest possible record of a day of joy and thanksgiving. Ten more years have gone, during which it will not be denied that Brunswick Church has been, in the main, true to its traditions;

and though it may not greatly have extended its influence, it has, at least, maintained its strength.

The Rev. Jabez Percival became the superintendent minister in 1888, joining the Rev. John Taylor, who had succeeded Mr. Hopkins in the previous year, and who, after four years' absence, has returned as pastor of the Heap Bridge section, where he is now engaged. Mr. Percival's sermons were of a popular character, and during the winter months special efforts were made to attract outsiders by means of evangelistic services, which were not without success. During his ministry the sum of £1,000 was raised for the new organ.

The movement towards this object originated with the chapel choir, who asked to be allowed to open an organ fund. The trustees thereupon took up the matter, following on similar lines to those which had been so successful in the great bazaar. A tea-meeting was held, at which the sympathies of the congregation were enlisted, and a considerable portion of the money required was promised by the trustees themselves. A ladies' committee was

appointed, with Miss E. Ashworth as secretary, and
Miss Lucy Ormerod as treasurer. After the great
enterprise of 1882, it was thought to be hardly in
accordance with the fitness of things to describe
the effort to raise so paltry a sum as £1,000 by the
term "bazaar." Accordingly, a "sale of work"
was opened in Brunswick School, on March 18th,
1891, by Alderman Cronshaw, Mayor of Heywood,
a member of our Church at Heap Bridge. The
desired amount was realized, and that without such
expedients as "raffles" or "mock auctions."

A small proportion of the above sum was spent in
providing for the better lighting and ventilation of
the chapel, and an organ committee proceeded to
make enquiries as to the purchase of a suitable
instrument. The persons comprising the committee
were Messrs. William Wild, J. Meadowcroft, Joseph
Ashworth, James Ashworth, James Holt, Sam
Smith, E. W. B. Smith, Edwin Smith, Cyrus
Hartley, and J. R. Barnes, secretary. It was
eventually decided to accept the tender of Mr.
George Benson, of Manchester, the total cost of the

organ, including gas engine, to be £1,115. The organ has three manuals, and contains thirty-five musical stops, together with the necessary couplers.

This "king of instruments" was opened with an organ recital by the late Irvine Dearnaley, Esq., of Ashton-under-Lyne, on September 14th, 1892. It is handsome in appearance, its internal construction and arrangement reflects the highest credit upon the builder, and it is entirely worthy of the place which it occupies. The opening services were continued on the three following Sundays, and were conducted by the Revs. John Adcock, John Truscott (President), and the circuit ministers.

Early in the term of the present minister, it was felt desirable that an alteration should be made in the constitution of the Leaders' Meeting, which is the executive body of the Church, so as to give it a more representative character. The meeting now combines the several important interests associated with the place, and includes representatives of the trustees and the Sunday school, together with certain delegates, who, in addition to the Church officers, are elected by the annual Church meeting.

. Various attempts have been made of late to develope the social life of the Church, so as to bring the members of the congregation into closer touch with each other. In February, 1893, a conversazione was organised on a large scale. Friends readily lent their pictures and curiosities, and the schoolroom was arrayed as a great drawing-room. The first day was set apart for the seat-holders, the second for teachers and elder scholars, and the third for the children. The proceedings were highly success-ful, and afforded much delight. For two successive winters "social evenings" have been held, which have resulted in the assembling of large numbers of friends. The series commenced in November, 1894, with an "at home" given by Mr. and Mrs. James Holt. Another similar entertainment was provided by Mr. and Mrs. Riley. There were also concerts, a lecture, and an organ recital. Last winter the movement was continued on a rather larger scale, and included, besides the features already mentioned, conversaziones given by the young men and women of the Sunday school. The aim which has always been kept in view in the organisation of these gatherings has been not only to provide a few hours of innocent enjoyment, but to afford more frequent opportunities of friendly intercourse between the members of the congregation, and so to strengthen that spirit of brotherly love which is essential to the life and health of a Church.

In November, 1893, Brunswick, for the second time, had the gratification of celebrating a Mayoral Sunday. Mr. John Ashworth, grandson and name-sake of one of the founders of the Church, himself a prominent member, a past circuit steward and superintendent of the Sunday school, was elected Mayor of the Borough. The customary procession of the Corporation officials and dignitaries proceeded from the Town Hall, headed by the 1st V. B. L. F. (the Heap Bridge) Band. The chapel was well filled, and the service was an enjoyable one. The choir, under the leadership of Alderman Meadowcroft, rendered suitable anthems, and a solo was sung by

Miss Lois Whittaker. The text of the sermon was Isaiah xxxii., 1, 2, the remarks of the preacher being directed to the importance of character in national and corporate life. The collection was on behalf of the Bury Dispensary Hospital, and amounted to £13.

In reading over the circuit minutes this singular fact discloses itself, that notwithstanding the prosperity of past years, and the comparative ease with which money could be raised for various purposes, the circuit fund, out of which the salaries and expenses of the ministers are paid, was in a chronic condition of debt. Of course the debts were always cleared off, from time to time, by such expedients as sales of work and special subscriptions, but owing to the loose system which prevailed, of each place in the circuit bringing what it could raise without effort, there was almost always a balance on the wrong side. During the itinerancy of the Rev. T. W. Townend a levy was placed upon each church, but as it was not strictly enforced, the fund continued to be in arrears. The burden fell on the mother church, whose funds were never in excess of the requirements.

In December, 1893, a sale of work was held, by means of which debts to the extent of £165 were cleared off the church and circuit funds, besides ·which, £150 was provided for the alteration and beautifying of the school premises.

Once free from debt, was it possible to remain so ? This question was answered by the adoption of a method of securing weekly contributions through numbered envelopes, the effect of which has been that, for the first time in the history of the church and circuit, for a period of two-and-a-half years these funds have been satisfactorily maintained.

Reference should be made to the visits of the two leading committees of the denomination. In June, 1893, the Foreign Missionary Committee held its sittings in Brunswick Chapel. About seventeen gentlemen from various parts of the country were hospitably entertained by the friends, and a public missionary meeting was held, the chairman of which was the Rev. John Truscott (President), the speakers

including the Revs. T. Wakefield (late of East
Africa), J. Barton (of Australia), and W. Howe (of
East Africa). In October, 1895, the Connexional
Committee were similarly entertained for the space
of three days, when about twenty-seven of the
leading men in Free Methodism were present.
Elaborate arrangements were made, with the indis-
pensable help of the ladies, to provide for the comfort
of the guests. A missionary demonstration was held
in connection with this visit. Alderman Hart, of
Birmingham, presided, and speeches were made by
the Revs. E. D. Cornish (Connexional Secretary),
W. R. Sunman (President), J. Cockin, of Truro,
and Alderman Snape. Music was discoursed by the
united choirs of the circuit, and it was the testimony
of some of the senior members that a more successful public meeting had never been held in Brunswick
Chapel.

Though the last few years may not have been
signalised by any striking spiritual success, yet the
Church has numerically held its own. Possibly
more progress might have been attained had there

been greater enterprise and devotion, but there is still cause for thankfulness to God that the labours of His servants in this direction have borne some fruit, and that a considerable number of young men and women have been led to join the Church. This fact of itself is full of promise for the future, and we may confidently hope that these will, in due time, take upon themselves the responsibilities that will fall to them, and with the divine blessing, the best traditions of Brunswick not only be maintained, but surpassed.

It will be observed that the writer is the first minister to have been invited to labour in the circuit for a term of five years. Though Free Methodism has no rule to limit the period of ministerial service, yet many of the older circuits have but slowly yielded to any modification of the old Methodist system of a three years' itinerancy. The present generation, however, is recognising the wisdom of continuing a suitable appointment, and, in the future, extended pastorates will probably be the rule rather than the exception.

It now remains to mention some of the leaders in Church life, who have been called to their reward during the period comprised in this chapter.

Mrs. E. C. A. ALLEN died May 11th, 1886. Her maiden name was Alsop, and she was born at Althorp, in Derbyshire, in the year 1832. When about sixteen years of age, she came to reside in Bury, and some years after commenced a school in Eden Street. She followed this occupation throughout her life, removing first to Spring Street and then to Union Square, as the necessities of her school required. In 1859, she was married to the late Jonas Allen. Mrs. Allen possessed a taste for literary composition, and wielded the pen of a ready writer. She was a frequent contributor to various periodicals, and published, in 1866, a volume of poems, to which she gave the title, "Echoes of Heart Whispers." The little book was dedicated to Mrs. Franklin Howorth, and in the preface the author thus

modestly set forth her aim:—" If any sentiment therein contained should add the least influence to the side of virtue, temperance, and piety, it will not be altogether in vain that these unpretending lays are launched on the sea of publicity." Some years afterwards she published a temperance tale, entitled " The Westons of Riverdale, or the Trials and Triumphs of Temperance Principles," and which she dedicated to the Earl of Shaftesbury. As a novel it was a very creditable performance, and has passed through several editions.

But Mrs. Allen's chief work, and that in which she took most delight, was in connection with Brunswick. She was a class leader from being twenty-one years of age, and for many years a teacher of the senior female Bible class in the Sunday school. She often gave public addresses, and was an earnest worker in the temperance cause. One of the last works of her life was the forming of a Band of Hope amongst the children at the workhouse.

During her later years she was a great sufferer,

but she bore her pain with admirable patience, and her calm and uncomplaining spirit was in itself a benediction. Her death took place almost instantaneously. Some premonition of it seems to have possessed her mind, for on the Sunday previous she had read the following lines of her own composition, to the members of her Sunday school class :—

### "IT SHALL BE WELL."

" Father ! this life that came from Thee
    Is in Thy keeping and Thy care ;
'Tis Thou alone its close canst see :
    The solemn *how*, or *when*, or *where*,
These eyes on earthly scenes shall close ;
    *I* know not, but my Father knows.

" *It may be in a moment's space ;*
    No time for parting words of sorrow ;
Caught up to see Thy smiling face
    In heaven's eternal, bright to-morrow.
That will be best for me, I know,
    If, Father, Thou shalt will it so.

" It may be with kind friends around,
    Who fain would keep me longer here ;
Who cannot hush the deep sob's sound,
    Who cannot check the gushing tear.

But Thou wilt heal the spirit's woe,
    For, Father, Thou hast promised so.

"It may be on the restless sea,
    Rocked to death's sleep upon the billow,
Some ocean cave my bed may be,
    The drifted weeds may be my pillow.
That will be right for me, I know,
    If, Father, Thou shalt will it so.

"It may be when, within the heart,
    Hope builds her bower and care sits lightest;
When round life's paths new beauties start,
    And earth is dressed in robes the brightest.
But, 'twill be right e'en then to go,
    If, Father, Thou dost will it so.

"It may be aged and alone,
    Life's wintry sky spread dark above me;
Left by my dear ones, one by one,
    None there to cherish, none to love me,
That Thou shalt call me from earth's woe.
    Well, Father! if Thou will'st it so.

"Safe in Thy loving care I rest,
    Whatever form of death may come,
Shall but obey Thy high behest,
    Thy messenger to take me home.
And 'tis enough for me to know
    That, Father, Thou dost will it so."

JOSEPH WELSBY belonged to a family which had been closely associated with the Methodist Free Church at Clitheroe. He greatly prized the traditions of the denomination, and was always ready to claim for its founders the honour of having rendered signal service to the cause of religious liberty. An ardent supporter of freedom both in Church and State, he would have suffered much rather than surrender the rights of conscience. He was a lover of books, and though not an omnivorous reader, was very familiar with some choice works of the best authors. Possibly this taste was induced by his occupation as a printer. In disposition he was genial, and his sprightliness, intelligence, and good nature, made him an agreeable companion. Possessed of a fine physical frame, his countenance, when in health, reflected the freshness of his spirit. For six years he held the office of circuit steward, and in that capacity he gained the friendship of the ministers with whom he was associated. He died June 10th, 1886, after a long and depressing illness.

RICHARD LORD was the son of John Lord, one of the leaders in the secession from Wesleyan Method-

ism in 1835. He joined the Church in early life, and filled many distinguished offices, such as class leader, Sunday school teacher, and superintendent. He was one of the first trustees, and held the office of circuit steward for fifteen years. As a man of business he was prompt and conscientious in all his engagements, and in proportion as he prospered in the world, so his generosity to the Church increased. He took a deep interest in the progress of the denomination, was a liberal supporter of the various Connexional institutions, and was several times elected as a representative to the Annual Assembly. His health had been failing for some time, but the end came somewhat suddenly, and he died January 9th, 1891, aged 75.

WILLIAM WILD, also one of the original trustees, and the son of one of the founders, passed away in

September of the same year. He was a devoted and an upright man, deeply attached to the Church, and spared neither time nor trouble in promoting its interests.

JOSEPH CLEMISHAW bore a name which had been associated with Brunswick from its commencement. He was a man of independent views, a generous supporter of the cause, and for some years served the Trust in the capacity of secretary. It was owing largely to his wisdom and promptitude, that the lease on which the premises are held was obtained from the lord of the manor on very favourable terms to the trustees. The death of his wife in January, 1893, affected him deeply, and in the May following he was laid beside her in the grave.

JOSEPH ROBINSON was one of the younger trustees. He earnestly devoted his energies to Christian work, and rendered useful service at Birtle and Limefield, where, as a teacher of young men, he was greatly beloved. His sun went down while it was yet day. He died in February, 1893, in the forty-second year of his age.

JAMES JOPSON had been a Sunday school teacher and superintendent for many years, and was a trustee, not only of Brunswick, but of other places in the circuit. His later years were spent in connection with our Church at Parkhills. He died August 12th, 1893.

WILLIAM ROBINSON, the younger, did not join the Church until his maturity, yet when he did so, he strove to atone for his lack of service in his earlier life. He possessed a remarkable gift of humour, and had the faculty of making both himself and others happy. He died in November, 1893. His only son FRANK, the last survivor of the family on the male side, died in his twenty-first year, in December, 1895. He was a young man of rare promise, one of the secretaries of the Sunday school, and his early death was much lamented.

SAMUEL BUTTERWORTH, who died November 3rd, 1893, was a plain, godly man, a lover of peace, and a consistent Christian. He was a trustee, and served the Church according to his ability.

GEORGE LORD ASHWORTH was also a trustee, and for many years a Sunday school teacher and superintendent. He was a quiet, unassuming man, slow of speech, but faithful in good works. He married a daughter of John Lord, and lived to a good old age. He died in January, 1894.

JAMES ASHWORTH is the last of the trustees who have been called away by death. This event took place, after a short illness, on January 4th, 1896, in his sixty-seventh year. Mr. Ashworth has held numerous offices, among which were those of superintendent of the Sunday school, chapel steward since 1867, and treasurer of the sick and burial society. In each of these positions he discharged his duties with the utmost fidelity. Upright and reliable in character, prompt in his engagements, wise in council, and kind in word and deed, he was a fine example of a Christian gentleman, and his place in the Church will be hard to fill.

JOHN WILD was a man of simple habits and sincere piety. A Methodist of the old-fashioned type, he loved the means of grace, and was usually

the first to lift up his voice in the prayer-meetings.
No one was more regular nor more devout in public
worship, and the preachers found in him a
sympathetic and appreciative hearer. Ardently
devoted to the temperance cause, he lost no
opportunity of recommending the advantages of
total abstinence. He died February 25th, 1896.

Few churches have been called upon, in so short
a period, to suffer losses so numerous and so great,
and besides these there have been many others
whose names are in the Book of Life, who served
God according to their gifts on earth, and who now
serve Him where His servants see His face. The
older generation has almost entirely disappeared ;
few indeed are the survivors of the first days, and
with these the period of active work is nearly over.
It is gratifying to know that in some cases the
saying is true that "instead of thy fathers shall be
thy children," and that the names of some of the
founders of the Church bid fair to be perpetuated in
the consecration of their descendants to the work of
God. Unfortunately the succession is not always

maintained, but so long as the Church is enterprising and aggressive, so long as the spirit of true Christian devotion and self-sacrifice remains, will a spiritual succession arise, to preserve all that is sacred of the past, and to hand on the inheritance, unimpaired in its strength and vigour, to coming generations.

# CHAPTER X.

## THE ORGANISATIONS.

---

"A yet nobler result of the religious revival was the steady attempt, which has never ceased from that day to this, to remedy the guilt, the ignorance, the physical suffering, the social degradation of the profligate and the poor. It was not till the Wesleyan impulse had done its work, that this philanthropic impulse began."

J. R. GREEN.

---

MOST of the organisations connected with Brunswick Church have been more or less referred to in the preceding chapters. A more detailed notice of some of them is however necessary, in order to furnish something like a complete account of its varied operations.

First and foremost is the SUNDAY SCHOOL. The circumstances under which it originated have already been described. The founders contended that they were not establishing a new Sunday school, but

merely transferring from one set of premises to
another, an institution which had grown up under
their management. This step, they argued, had
been forced upon them through the imposition of
new regulations, about which they had never been
consulted, and to which they declined to submit.
In harmony with this position, they sent in a claim
for three-fourths of the library in Clerke Street
School, which they succeeded in obtaining.

In their new premises they continued to carry out
the same discipline as before. They elected their
own officers and committee, half-yearly, and arranged
their own curriculum, the Wesleyan Catechism being
used in the upper classes; writing was taught for
some years, and "writing masters" were regularly
appointed along with the officers of the school. New
furniture and books were of course required, and
donations were publicly solicited for that object.
The ready response with which the appeal was met
will be seen from the handsome subscription list
which was presented at the first anniversary.

In June, 1836, a school at the Hinds sought the

assistance and association of that in the "Tabernacle," and for several years it was considered as a branch school, and supplied with teachers.

In September, a week-night school was opened for boys, for which a supply of pens, ink, paper, and candles was ordered to be provided out of the Sunday school funds.

In November of the same year it was arranged for certain teachers to attend the school every Sunday, from twelve to two o'clock, for the purpose of preventing damage being done to the property.

On Good Friday, in 1837, the chapel in North Street was opened for public worship, and on the morning of that day the scholars marched in procession to their new schoolroom, where an address was delivered to them by Joseph Green.

The anniversary services were at first held on Whit-Sunday, as at Union Street, but eventually the date was altered, and after varying for several years, the last Sunday in April was selected, and has been used ever since. The singing at the earlier anniversaries was conducted by John Ashworth, who was assisted in his training of the children by James Mills and Henry Dearden. In 1842, this duty was assigned to William Wild and Daniel Smith, afterwards to Daniel Smith and John Lord, so long as the latter was able to render service. Daniel Smith was next assisted by Peter Ormerod, and, in course of time, by Mr. Jesse Meadowcroft. For twenty-nine years, from 1863 to 1892, Mr. Meadowcroft fulfilled this honourable but onerous task single-handed, and upon his relinquishing the responsibility through failing health, it fell first upon Mr. William Mitchell for two years, and latterly on Mr. W. A. Stock, the present master of the Sunday school choir. Upon the twenty-fifth occasion of Mr. Meadowcroft's leadership, in 1888, he was made the recipient of an illuminated address and a gold-mounted baton, from the officers and teachers of the school, in recognition of his generous and ungrudging services in that capacity.

A list of the preachers on these occasions is furnished in an appendix, together with the amount of the collections. It will be there seen that for

fifteen years the morning address was delivered by
John Ashworth, of Rochdale, the famous author of
" Strange Tales from Humble Life." This was
always a very popular appointment, the humour and
pathos of the speaker, joined with the splendid
story-telling faculty which he knew so well how to
use, always ensuring a crowded chapel.

Many were the " strange tales " which John Ashworth told during these addresses, but none were
listened to with more delight than those in which he
related the struggles and privations of his early life,
and how his mother, who was a pious woman, sent him
to Sunday school for the first time without shoes or
stockings, his patched garments covered by a pack-
sheet pinafore, with half the letters " Wool " down
on one side of it, to take his place beside boys much
better dressed, who ungenerously looked down upon
him because of his poverty, and cruelly trod upon
his bare toes. Nor were his audiences ever tired of
hearing how he bore all this uncomplainingly, and
that he won the highest prize given in the school.

John Ashworth had a deep-rooted objection to

railway travelling on Sundays, and invariably performed the journey from Rochdale to Bury and back on foot.

Mention should be made of certain auxiliary organisations, which the Sunday school has called into existence from time to time.

There has been a Sick and Burial Society in connection with the Sunday school from its commencement. By weekly payments, varying according to age, any scholar, teacher, or member of the congregation may make suitable provision for sickness or death, in the same way as in other similar friendly societies. The "sick list," as it is called, was instituted on February 21st, 1836, the first officers being Joseph Ashworth, secretary, and Robert Collins, treasurer. The operations of the society have been somewhat diminished owing to the multiplication of such organisations in recent years, nevertheless it is in a very sound financial condition, and in the course of its existence has been of unspeakable benefit to many families in times of sickness and bereavement. The last report states that there are 138 members, and that its accumulated funds amount to £1,265 0s. 10½d. The late James Ashworth held the office of treasurer for many years. Mr. William Foulds is the secretary.

In 1860 a School Missionary was employed for the purpose of visiting sick and absent scholars and teachers. It was also arranged that a part of his duty should be to read the burial service at interments, in recognition of which the trustees should contribute a portion of his salary. This office was first held by Hugh Kelly, and next by Mr. John Ashton, who is still a useful local preacher in the circuit. Since the year 1869 Mr. John Smith has regularly performed these functions, and in his visitations of the sick and dying has been the means of leading many to Christ. He has also served the circuit as a local preacher. In the discharge of these varied duties for so long a period he has earned a widespread regard.

An Adult Bible Class was established in January, 1886. It is conducted on the lines of the " Pleasant Sunday Afternoon " movement, prizes being given for regular attendance, and is attended by many who would otherwise have long ceased their connection with the Sunday school.

The Young People's Society of Christian Endeavour held its first meeting on June 6th, 1894. Since then it has assembled uninterruptedly on Wednesday evenings, and has proved itself a valuable connecting link between the school and the Church.

On the last two Christmas mornings a Free Breakfast has been given to between four and five hundred poor children, by the scholars and teachers of the school. The amount of enthusiasm that has been thrown into the work, and the evident pleasure that it has afforded to those who have taken part in it, give promise that the breakfast will become an annual institution.

To tell the story of all that has been accomplished by Brunswick Sunday School, and of the godly men and women who have laboured in it, would require a volume in itself, but the school has always remained so closely identified with the Church, that the

history of the one is to a very large extent that of
the other. Although several branch schools have
been established in the neighbourhood, all of which
have drawn more or less of their strength from it,
yet it has maintained its numbers, and may still
claim to be the premier Nonconformist school of the
district, while in point of its average attendance, and
in the number of its teachers and workers, it stands
second to none in the town. Its young people have
always been foremost in good works, and ready to
assist in any enterprise for the welfare of the Church.

Next in order of thought, though not in order of
time, is the DAY SCHOOL. In the year 1859 the
trustees expressed their opinion that day schools
ought to be erected in connection with the chapel,
and placed under Government inspection. That
desire was supplanted by the movement on behalf of
a new chapel, and it was not till January, 1870, that
an infant school was started and placed under the
care of Miss Blakeley. Twelve months later a mixed
school was established.

GEORGE WENSLEY was the first head-master.
He was a Lancashire man and a Free Methodist,
having been a member of the Church at Hyde
Road, Manchester. He not only diligently performed his scholastic duties, but became also a local
preacher and Sunday school teacher, and entered
heartily into the whole work of the Church. For a
time he was missionary secretary to the circuit. In
the fulfilment of that office he displayed much ardour,
attending to the various details of the organisation, visiting regularly the various churches and
schools, until the missionary contributions rose to
over £100 a year, once reaching as high as £150.
He also gave himself to philanthropic work in the
town, and was largely instrumental in establishing
the Hospital Saturday movement in Bury, in recognition of which he was given a place on the hospital
committee. Unfortunately his physical strength was
not equal to his desire to do good, and he died on
December 22nd, 1885, at the early age of forty-four,
having been master of Brunswick School for
fifteen years. On his tombstone in the chapel

cemetery has been inscribed the epitaph, which is perfect in its truth and appropriateness, " He spent himself for God and man."

For the next four years the school was under the charge of Mr. C. S. Cook, who was succeeded by the present master, Mr. Isaac Ingham, in whose hands the school has attained a very high degree of efficiency and success. The infant department has been under the capable management of Miss Kate Walter since 1890. The school board is subject to election by the Sunday school teachers' meeting. The close union of these two institutions will justify the quotation of the lines of Whittier :—

> " Nor heeds the sceptic's puny hands
>   While near the school the church-spire stands ;
>   Nor fears the blinded bigot's rule,
>   While near her church-spire stands her school."

The Dorcas Society was instituted as early as the year 1837, " for the poor of all denominations in Bury and its vicinity." Its aims were announced in the following circular :—

## DORCAS SOCIETY.

"Plead the cause of the poor and needy."

The object of this society is to provide plain and suitable clothing for gratuitous distribution amongst poor, afflicted, and aged persons; and the society is more particularly prompted to do this, on account of the cold and inclement season that is approaching, when clothing is so essential to health and comfort.

To accomplish this laudable object, the society respectfully solicits the assistance of the Christian public, either in subscriptions, donations, or work, as may be most convenient and agreeable.

President of the society, Mrs. Fishwick; Treasurer, Mrs. Ashworth; Secretary, Miss Fishwick; Committee, Mrs. Lord, Mrs. Jones, Mrs. Siddell, Mrs. Holt, Mrs. Fishwick, Mrs. Potts; Purchasers and Cutters-out, Mrs. Fishwick, Mrs. Lord, Mrs. Holt; Collectors, Mrs. Potts, Mrs. Ashworth, Miss Fishwick, Miss Clemishaw, Mrs. Fishwick.

No person to be relieved without being first visited by one of the members.

*October 21st, 1837.*

This useful society has met month by month, except in summer, since its inauguration, and has enlisted the co-operation of the ladies of the congregation. Its annual reports are records of benevolent deeds, and though its income has never been great, yet its ministry, like that of Dorcas of old, has been fraught with blessings to the poor and the fatherless. The names of the ladies associated with it are familiar as household words in the history of Brunswick. The income for the past year was £20 10s. 3d., and the number of articles distributed was 225. The officers are, Mrs. Fethney, president; Mrs. Stock, vice-president; Mrs. Welsby, treasurer; and Miss H. Lord, secretary.

The BRUNSWICK TEMPERANCE SOCIETY was established in 1849, and next to the Bury Abstinence Society it is the oldest temperance organisation in the town. The first committee consisted of James Riley, president; Robert Bleasdale, treasurer; Henry Jefferson, secretary; Richard Lord, Joshua Lord, Joseph Fletcher, junior, Isaac Smith, James Ashworth, Jacob Fletcher, George Hargreaves, John Ormerod, and William Barlow. In the earlier days of its existence a vigorous propaganda was carried on, lectures on temperance and other subjects were

organised, and the society exerted a powerful
influence in the locality. In 1858, under the joint
secretaryship of Messrs. Lambert Fletcher and John
Ashworth, free lectures were given by Joseph Petrie,
Esq., of Rochdale, the Revs. W. Stott, A. Gilbert,
John Peters, S. Macfarlane, and others, which were
attended by crowded audiences. Popular lecturers
like Dr. Lees, Thomas Hacking, Marmaduke Miller,
and John Guttridge, were also secured. In 1862 a
mission was held in various parts of the town and
neighbourhood, during which Messrs. J. Stockdale,
J. Ashton, J. Ashworth, and J. Wild, addressed
enthusiastic gatherings, Mr. J. Meadowcroft provided the music, and one hundred and ten persons
signed the pledge. These instances might easily
be multiplied, but they are sufficient to show
the character of the society's operations in its most
flourishing period. A Band of Hope has been
worked in connection with it, from time to time, in
which large numbers of young people have been
instructed in temperance principles. The society
also catered for the public at Whitsuntide and

other holidays, by arranging for excursions to places of popular resort, so much so that it may be said to have been the pioneer of railway trips from Bury. Though it is still in existence, the society cannot, of course, be expected to display the enterprise that characterized its earlier history, inasmuch as the greater part of the work which it attempted is now better done by other and more general organisations. Mr. William Holt is president of the society, Mr. Arthur Holt secretary, and Mr. E. W. B. Smith treasurer.

The CHAPEL CHOIR. The musical arrangements at Brunswick Chapel have been in comparatively few hands from the commencement. John Lord was the first choirmaster, and held the office until his death, in 1852. He was succeeded by Daniel Smith, the second son of David Smith.

Daniel Smith's chief service to Brunswick was rendered in connection with the choir. He was extremely fond of music, and a creditable player upon the violin. He rarely took part in Church

N

affairs outside this particular sphere, though his
purse was always open for the support of its various
institutions. He was a man of
an altogether different type to
his two brothers. Of a retiring
disposition and of few words,
he shrank from public offices,
and spent most of his spare
time at home. He had a good
deal of dry humour, seldom laughed, and was
inclined to be caustic in speech. The death of his
brother Samuel affected him deeply, and when a
deputation from the young women's class came to
invite him to fill the vacancy caused by that event,
he was persuaded to become a Sunday school
teacher. This work was to him a great trial, but
so long as he was able he did it, and did it well.
He survived his elder brother about ten years, and
died in 1879.

Another name closely associated with Brunswick
choir from the beginning is that of Peter Ormerod.
In the days of fiddles he played the double-bass,

and when these were relegated to the past, he
remained in the choir as a tenor singer. For a
number of years he assisted in the training of the
children for the school anniversaries, his duty being
to teach the lads to sing alto. He was also a class
leader, and served the Church in a variety of ways,
at one time performing the functions of society
steward. While the new chapel was in course of
erection, business called him to leave the town, and
he resided at Shaw until his death, which took place
on June 28th, 1892. He was buried in Brunswick
Cemetery. His widow, who was a sister of Daniel
Smith, is still living, and though connected with the
Wesleyan Church, retains much of her former
affection for Brunswick.

Mr. Jesse Meadowcroft became deputy leader in
the closing years of Daniel Smith's occupancy, and
when the latter died, succeeded him in the position,
which he held until his resignation, owing to
physical weakness, in the beginning of 1895. When
that event took place, it was recognised in a fitting
manner by the leaders, who presented Mr.

Meadowcroft with an illuminated address, gratefully acknowledging the value of his services cheerfully and gratuitously rendered for so many years.

In the earlier years the singing was accompanied by stringed instruments, these giving place to the organ in the year 1855. Mr. David Smith was designated as the first organist, but as he was a youth at school when the organ was built, he was put in training, and the duty was performed for a time by the late J. Randle Fletcher and W. E. Spragg. Mr. David Smith continued to play for some time after he had left Bury to take up his residence in Heywood. He was succeeded by Mr. Edwin Smith, whose resignation, in 1880, was received with much regret by the trustees. During the latter part of Mr. Edwin's time he was assisted by his cousin, Mr. Samuel Smith (David's brother), with whom he took alternate services. Up to this period no salary had been paid in connection with the choir. In 1880 Mr. E. W. B. Smith was appointed at a small remuneration. He was followed by Mr. Cyrus Hartley, in 1884, and he again, in 1891, by Mr. W. S. Smith. Mr. Meadowcroft's resignation as choirmaster was accompanied by that of the organist, and in March, 1895, Mr. J. T. Schofield was selected for the joint position.

The old organ was a comparatively small instrument, almost without frame, and exhibiting the metal pipes. A few years after its introduction, a new frame was purchased, and the organ was enlarged to fill it. It underwent numerous enlargements and improvements, frequently made at the expense of Daniel Smith, and it was eventually placed in the new chapel, where it remained until the fine instrument described in the preceding chapter was erected, in 1892.

THE CEMETERY. The first interment in the cemetery attached to Brunswick Chapel, was that of the infant daughter of the late Thomas Holt, who died February 6th, 1837. Conveyances were then rarely used, except among wealthier folk, and it was part of the sexton's duty to take the bier to the house where the corpse lay, that the coffin might be

carried from there to its last resting place. For this
service he was entitled to make a charge of sixpence
when the distance lay beyond Bury Bridge, Heap
Bridge, Huntley Brook, Buckley Wells, or Limefield.
Many funerals took place on Sunday afternoons.
This greatly interfered with the public services,
which were then held three times on the Sunday,
and in 1851, the trustees thought it advisable to
close the chapel in the afternoon, so that suitable
arrangements might be made for interments. The
duty of reading the burial service rested upon the
ministers, and took up a considerable portion of
their time, but they were at length relieved by the
appointment of a school missionary.

When the Cemeteries Act was passed it was feared
that its effect would be to close the Brunswick graveyard, but upon petition it was allowed to remain
open, together with the graveyards belonging to
St. Paul's Church and Elton Church.

The functions of sexton and chapel-keeper have,
except for a brief interval, been performed by one and
the same person. The names of the various chapel-

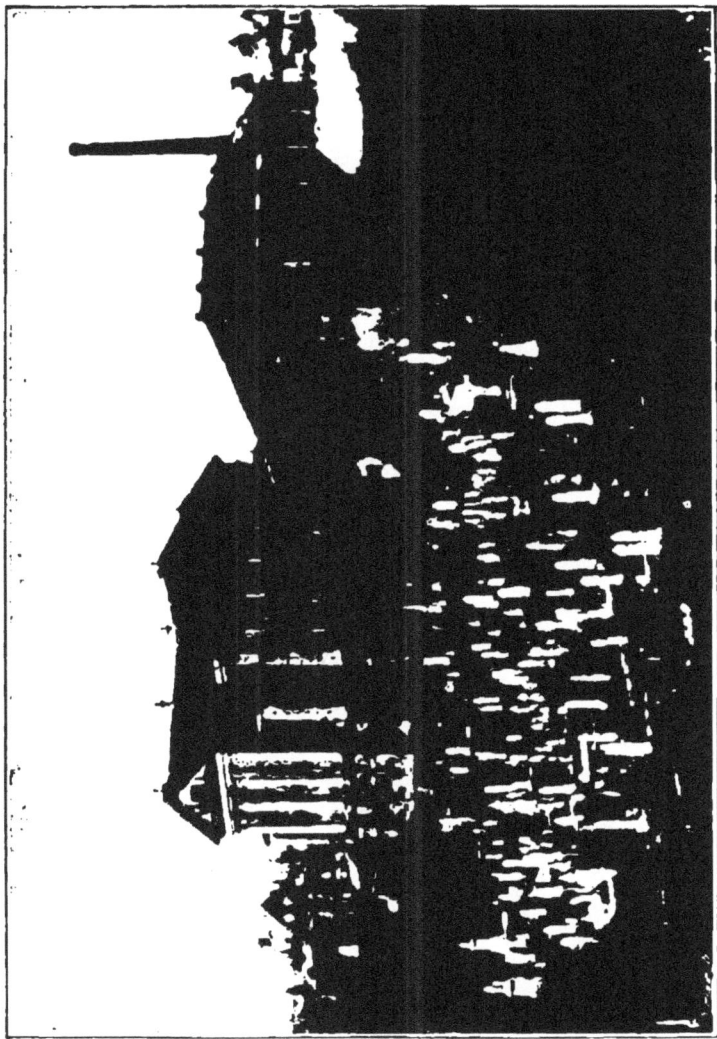

BRUNSWICK CEMETERY.

keepers are Christopher Huddlestone, Charles Dawson, who was a class leader and a man of considerable mental power, Mark Hargreaves from 1873, and George Cordingley from 1892. In our photograph of the new chapel the familiar figure of Mark Hargreaves may be seen standing near the gate.

Many names of persons who have been closely associated with Brunswick Church and School are to be found on the tombstones in the cemetery; and of most of the departed who are referred to in the foregoing pages, their mortal remains lie buried under the shadow of the Church they loved.

In addition to these, there may be seen the graves of William Buckley, formerly of Deeply Vale, and afterwards of Horwich, whose widow followed him in three months, having died, it is said, of a broken heart; Samuel Grundy, solicitor, of Bury; William Tuer, founder of the present firm of Robert Hall and Sons; John Howard, of Accrington, senior partner in the great concern of Howard and Bullough; Benjamin Crapper; Thomas Hampton, town missionary; John Cronshaw, one of the original members of our Church at Heap Bridge; the Rev. William Roseman, for many years minister at Castlecroft Congregational Church; Richard Butcher, travelling secretary to the Religious Tract Society; and Lillian and Nellie, daughters of the Rev. W. R. Sunman.

# CHAPTER XI.

## THE CIRCUIT.

"It is the aim of each visible Church, and each congregation of faithful men, first to have life in itself, and then to kindle life where it is not; to make continual inroads upon outlying unrighteousness until the Church and the World become one and the same."

J. HAMILTON THOM.

BRUNSWICK Church is at present the head of a circuit which comprises eight congregations and Sunday schools.

At first, as has been shown, Bury formed a portion of the extensive and powerful Rochdale Circuit, one of whose ministers, the Rev. Joseph Handley, resided in this town. In 1840 it was deemed advisable that a partition should be made, and the "Bury and Bolton Circuit" was constituted at the Annual Assembly of that year. Since then the circuit has been twice divided. First in 1847, when Bolton had become strong enough to stand alone. The Bury Circuit then only contained two chapels, namely, Brunswick and Ramsbottom, with preaching rooms at Heap Bridge, Burrs, and Besses o'th' Barn, and cottage meetings held on week-nights at Hutchinson's Row and Woolfold. The names of the preachers, taken from a plan of that date, were W. H. Walker (minister), J. Lord, J. Green, E. Potts, P. Hall, J. Hargreaves, J. Riley, S. Cook, J. Fletcher, I. Smith, J. Grindrod, F. Alsop; on trial, S. Campbell, J. Sperritt. About the year 1849 Woodhill and Limefield were added to the list of preaching places.

When Mr. Mather came to the circuit, in 1852, there were three chapels—Brunswick, Ramsbottom, and Heap Bridge; preaching was also held at Limefield on Sunday evenings, and on occasional week-nights, with a fortnightly service at Burrs, Woodhill, and Shaw's Row. In 1853 a cause was commenced at Radcliffe, which continued until the period of the cotton famine, when it was given up owing to the removal of the leading members from the neighbourhood. In the meantime there had

been added to the preachers' plan the names of A.
Taylor, J. Bromley, T. Taylor, H. Cooper, J. Ramsbottom, and H. Brown.

The second division took place in 1871, when
the churches at Ramsbottom and Hawkshaw Lane
were formed into a new circuit, which has since been
enlarged by the addition of a cause at Holcombe
Brook.

We may now describe briefly the origin and
progress of the smaller churches which at present
constitute the Bury Circuit.

## HEAP BRIDGE.

The cause at Heap Bridge commenced almost
contemporaneously with that of Brunswick. Its
name appears on the Rochdale plan for 1837 as a
place for afternoon preaching only. There were two
society classes, led by Thomas Jones and James
Mather. The society must have attained a moderate
degree of strength towards the end of 1838, for we
then find the Brunswick Sunday School consenting
to the loan of its " thrustles " to the Heap Bridge

friends for the purpose of a tea-party. At first the meetings of the church and school were held in a cottage at Old Hand, then in a room at the paper mill, but afterwards the friends were granted the free use of the school belonging to Edmund Grundy, Esq., a member of the Unitarian body, The only survivor of the early workers is Mr. Abraham Whittaker, of Halifax.

The foundation stone of the first chapel was laid on August 6th, 1851, and the Revs. J. Molineux and A. Gilbert are named in connection with the proceedings. The building cost £400, and when it was opened by the Rev. Thomas Hacking, on the Christmas Day of the same year, £260 of this amount had been raised. The work was blessed with considerable spiritual success, so that larger premises were soon required.

The present chapel was commenced in the year 1866, the corner stone being laid by Charles Cheetham, J.P., of Heywood, on November 3rd. It was opened for public worship in April, 1868, by the Rev. John Guttridge. The building was designed and its erection superintended by Mr. John Cronshaw, J.P. Its cost was defrayed partly by subscription, and partly by a bazaar held in the Bury Athenæum, in 1873, which was opened by Daniel Smith. It has been since enlarged by the addition of new class-rooms and other conveniences necessary to fit it for Sunday and day school purposes. The chapel contains a marble tablet erected to the memory of John Cronshaw, senior, who was for many years treasurer to the Trust, a prominent leader of the Church, and a useful Sunday school teacher. He died on June 17th, 1880, in his seventieth year. The organ, which is a fine instrument, bears this inscription:—" Presented by Alderman and Mrs. Cronshaw, May 18th, 1890." Mr. John Cronshaw was Mayor of Heywood for two successive years. On the first Sunday after his election to that office, in November, 1890, he attended service with the Corporation, in Heap Bridge Chapel, the Rev. S. Poad being the preacher on that occasion.

In 1889 an arrangement was made with the circuit, whereby the Heap Bridge Church should have the greater part of the labours of a minister. The Rev. Samuel Poad was invited, and he served the Church with considerable credit and success for a period of four years. He was succeeded by the Rev. John Taylor, who has thus passed a second term of three years in the Bury Circuit.

## LIMEFIELD.

In 1849 the quarterly meeting determined to commence a preaching service in a cottage in this village, "if the parties be agreeable and of good character." A branch school was opened in 1854, in a cottage in How Lane, and the little place was soon filled with children. Few persons, however, attended the preaching, on account of the inconvenience of the accommodation that was provided. There being no other Nonconformist place of worship in the locality, a plot of land was secured, and steps taken towards the erection of a suitable building. Joseph Hacking drew up the plans and specifications, and it was stipulated that the erection should not cost more than £200. The Rev. John

Mather laid the foundation stone, and a very neat and substantial chapel was opened on December 9th, 1855, the preachers on the occasion being the Rev. John Peters, superintendent minister, and the Rev. Aaron Weston, of Manchester. The enterprise proved very successful, the school increased in numbers, the congregations were good, and the building was consecrated by many conversions to God. The premises have since been enlarged and class-rooms added. Better accommodation is, however, needed, and through the persistent energy of scholars and friends a considerable sum of money has been raised towards a chapel and school, for which a new site has been secured near the Bury Dispensary Hospital. The ceremony of cutting the first sod was performed by Alderman Meadowcroft, in the presence of a considerable number of spectators, on June 27th, 1896, and building operations for the new school have already commenced.

## WARTH.

This church and school commenced in a room at

Bank Top, near Radcliffe, about the year 1854,
mainly owing to the instrumentality of Robert
Howarth, to whose memory a marble tablet has
been placed inside the present chapel. On July
31st, 1869, the corner stone of a chapel was laid on
the opposite side of the railway from the village of
Warth Fold, the ceremony being performed by
Richard Lord. Mr. J. H. Riley prepared the plans
and specifications, and the building, which cost
£640, was opened for Divine worship on Wednesday,
February 16th, 1870, by the Rev. John Adcock. In
consequence of mining operations in connection
with the colliery of Messrs. Knowles and Sons,
which penetrated beneath the land on which the
chapel was built, the foundations began to show
signs of subsidence, ominous cracks revealing
themselves in the walls, and it was feared the
structure would collapse. On the case being made
known to the colliery proprietors, they offered some
compensation for the damage done to the building,
which, however, barely sufficed to clear off the
balance of the chapel debt. This was a serious

position for a handful of working men and women
to face, but they bravely resolved to commence
anew.   The site was changed to the Warth side
of the railway, and the memorial stones of the
present chapel and school were laid on July 14th,
1888, by Mrs. Riley, Miss Ormerod (of Southport),
Mrs. J. Meadowcroft, Mr. Edwin Smith, and Mr.
Samuel Smith.   The building, which is a handsome
structure, cost upwards of £1,300, and was opened
on February 12th, 1889, by the Rev. Silas K.
Hocking.

There was a very heavy burden of debt remaining,
but through unwearied efforts and much self-sacrifice
it has been gradually reduced to more manageable
dimensions.   Both Sunday school and Church are
now in a flourishing condition, and Zion Chapel,
Warth, proportionately to its size, will compare
favourably with any other place in the circuit.

## ELTON.

The origin of Mount Pleasant School, Wood
Street, Elton, may be traced to some cottage services

held in 1858, at Richard Holden's, Crostons Road.
Early in the following year a cottage in Victoria
Street was rented, where a Sunday school was
commenced and public worship conducted for more
than eight years. On Whit-Friday, 1866, the
foundation stone of a substantial stone chapel,
in the Gothic style of architecture, was laid on
the side of what was then a country road. The
building was opened on October 17th, 1867, by
the Rev. Richard Chew, President of the Annual
Assembly. There was then no other place of
worship in Elton with the exception of the
Established Church. The locality increased in
population, new streets were laid out in the neighbourhood, the cause prospered, and in course of time
the premises were entirely free of debt. A day school
was commenced on August 30th, 1880, which became
so successful that it was found necessary to extend
the accommodation. An infant school and class
rooms were therefore added in 1884, and were soon
filled with scholars. Though the day school has
met the educational needs of the neighbourhood, yet

its effect upon the Church has not been altogether
a beneficial one. A room used for day school
purposes is not the most attractive as a place
of worship, and the want of such a place is
keenly felt. The outlay upon the enlargements,
however, proved to be greater than was at first
contemplated, the expense of working the place
was considerable, and the Trust found itself
encumbered with a formidable debt of about £1,900.
It was not till the year 1891 that any serious
attempt was made to lessen this burden, but since
then, by successive " sales of work," aided by the
liberal donations of trustees and friends, and by a
free loan of £250 from the Connexional Chapel
Fund, which is repayable by regular instalments,
the debt has been somewhat diminished, and it is
anticipated that in a few years' time it will have
ceased to be oppressive. The spiritual history of the
Church has been a variable one; there is, however,
a large Sunday school, and an earnest band of
devoted workers. Through the energy of Mr. J.

F. Timpany, a successful P.S.A. has been conducted
for several winters.

## BIRTLE.

Mount Tabor Chapel, Birtle, was commenced in
1862, when a few persons at Moulding requested to
be received into fellowship with the circuit. Several
young men from Brunswick came forward to assist
in the work. A substantial chapel was built in
1864, and for a time the cause flourished. But the
closing of the mill at Birtle Dean, which afforded
employment to a considerable number of people,
greatly reduced the population of the locality, and
both school and congregation are now very small.
Those who remain are deeply attached to the place,
and some who now live in Bury perform the journey
to Birtle every Sunday, displaying great fidelity and
self-denial in support of the cause they love.

## HIGHER WOODHILL.

This locality has been at various times missioned
by the circuit, and in the earlier years society

classes and preaching services were held in cottages at Burrs and Woodhill. The present Sunday school is conducted in a room built for the purpose, and belonging to Messrs. Yates Brothers, of Higher Woodhill Mill, whose kindness deserves mention. Public worship is also held on Sunday evenings. The place is dependent to a large extent upon the help it obtains from Brunswick.

## PARKHILLS.

In the year 1881 attention was drawn to the rapidly-growing suburb of Fishpool, as affording a suitable opening for the establishment of a cause in that locality. A committee was appointed by the quarterly meeting, for the purpose of making inquiries, but some time elapsed before any practical steps were taken. In 1883 a larger and stronger committee was formed, and progress at once commenced. The foundation stones of a neat school-chapel were laid on June 2nd, 1883, by Mrs. S. Smith, Mrs. Meadowcroft, Mrs. Joseph Allen, and the late Mr. Adam Ashworth, and the building was

opened on November 11th, in the same year, by the
Rev. Henry Holgate.   In connection with the event
a sermon was also preached in Brunswick Chapel,
about a fortnight after, by the Rev. Dr. Macfadyen.
The Sunday school was immediately established,
and a day school commenced on December 3rd.

The formation of the cause at Parkhills was not
accomplished without loss to Brunswick.   It resulted
in the withdrawal of several well-to-do families,
whose residences made it more convenient for them
to attend the new church, and it also furnished a
sphere of labour for a number of young men whose
energies had not been fully employed in the larger
place.

It was felt desirable from the first that Parkhills
should have the management of its own internal
affairs, and in 1884 it was constituted a separate
section of the circuit, and granted the privilege of
inviting its own minister.   Its choice fell upon the
Rev. John Mather, who at that time, in consequence
of his advancing years, was seeking a smaller pastorate than he had hitherto held.   To the gratification

of the entire circuit, Mr. Mather accepted the invitation, and commenced his labours in August, 1886. He served the Church for three years with considerable success, and then decided to retire from the regular ministry, still continuing to reside in Bury, and rendering valuable help not only to Parkhills, but to other places in the circuit. Mr. Mather was followed by a probationer, the Rev. J. W. Davies, and he, again, by the Rev. J. Herbert Shaw. In 1892, the Church finding it somewhat difficult to maintain a minister, requested Mr. Mather again to take the pastoral oversight, and to preach as often as might be convenient, and this arrangement is at present in force.

The Church at Parkhills suffered considerable losses consequent upon the removal of the railway works from Bury, but it is now showing signs of vigorous life : the Sunday school has grown almost beyond the capacity of the building, and the congregations are very good. There is an earnest band of young men and women, who are possessed with a truly evangelistic zeal, and the outlook is exceedingly bright. Liberal promises have been made in aid of the erection of a new chapel to face Parkhills Road, and, given suitable and commodious premises, there seems nothing likely to prevent this society from growing into a strong and flourishing Church. When that work is accomplished, it will form a fitting memorial of the useful life and devoted labours of the Rev. John Mather.

### LOCAL PREACHERS IN 1896.

| | |
|---|---|
| Henry Brown. | W. S. Berry. |
| John Ashton. | William Lord. |
| Lambert Fletcher. | James Dixon. |
| J. K. Lord. | W. Pemberton. |
| John Smith. | James Willis. |
| John Allen. | J. H. Park. |
| J. Priestley. | J. Wilkinson. |
| Robert Jackson. | J. F. Timpany. |
| E. W. B. Smith. | Peter Turner. |

Fred Shaw.

# CHAPTER XII.

## CONCLUSION.

"It is the highest pleasure that a man can have who has turned down the hill at last, to believe that younger spirits will rise up after him, and catch the lamp of truth, as in the old lamp-bearing race of Greece, out of his hand before it expires, and carry it on to the goal with swifter and more even feet."

CHARLES KINGSLEY.

THE real history of any church cannot be written with the pen of man. Its noblest achievements are not to be found in its bricks and mortar, nor in its financial and statistical records. These are only the scaffolding of the spiritual temple, the living stones of which are the godly men and women whose lives and characters have been built upon the one foundation, Jesus Christ. Its true record is inscribed in heaven's archives, and not until the day when the books of God shall be opened will it be made manifest.

We have attempted to relate the story of the origin and growth of Brunswick Church. We have seen how it has spread its branches in many directions, and become the nursing mother to other like communities. We have marked its influence upon the benevolent and philanthropic work of the town and neighbourhood. But this is not all. Vast numbers of people have, from time to time, formed its congregations, thousands of scholars have passed through its Sunday school. Many of these are now before the throne of God, and imagination can picture them as they serve Him day and night in the Heavenly Temple. "Glorious things are spoken of thee, O city of God," sang the psalmist, and the most glorious thing was, that this and that man was born to a new life in Zion. And of Brunswick it may be truly said, that

> " in the great decisive day,
> When God the nations shall survey,
> It will before the world appear
> That crowds were born to glory here."

Many, however, are now living, who owe their religious training, and their first impulses towards the Christian life, to this Church and school. Some of these are connected with other religious organisations, and far and wide, in various cities and towns of our own country, and in lands across the seas, the labours of God's servants here are bearing fruit. There has been, it must be owned, a sad leakage ; some who have been associated with this place in early life, have lapsed into religious indifference. But even of these we would not utterly lose hope, and would fain believe that some memory of the happy days they spent in the Sunday school and at the house of God, at times returns to them, to rebuke them for their worldliness, and to whisper its precious promise of the life which may yet be theirs.

Brunswick has never been a wealthy Church, although at one time it may have contained more well-to-do persons in its congregation than it does to-day. A very unpretentious, community in its earlier history, it gradually improved in social standing. The majority of its leading members have belonged to the trading class. There have been, however, those who followed more ambitious

pursuits. James Livesey was a cotton manufacturer;
the Ashworths are hat manufacturers; Tuer and
Halls, the Hackings, Downhams, Burgoines, Rileys,
were or are engineers; the founder of the great
engineering firm of Howard and Bullough, of
Accrington, was a son of Brunswick; Samuel and
Daniel Smith were interested in the cotton trade,
though the former was a draper, and the latter a
corn merchant; Henry Moorhouse was a civil
engineer, and though the latter portion of his life
was largely spent abroad, he continued to love and
support the cause he had served in his youth.
Most of these had small beginnings, and they are
representative of the persevering and indomitable
characteristics which have been distinguishing
features in Lancashire middle-class life.

In the public life of the town Brunswick has been
creditably represented.  Previous to the incorporation
of the borough, it had two town's Commissioners,—
Samuel Smith and Thomas Holt.   Since then it has
had two mayors—Robert Hall and Mr. John Ashworth ; three aldermen,—Messrs. J. Ashworth, Jesse

Meadowcroft, and Christopher Talbot. In addition to the above, the following are or have been Councillors:—Messrs. Thomas Ormerod, J. H. Riley, James Holt, and Lambert Fletcher. Messrs. Ashworth, Meadowcroft, and Cornelius Farrer are magistrates. Among its ministers, no less than eight have been Presidents of the Annual Assembly, two of them twice, and others beside these have sat upon Connexional Committees.

An eminent statesman has said that "the decisive sign of the elevation of a nation's life is to be sought among those who lead or ought to lead." And the character of a church is to a very large extent that of its leading men. In this respect Brunswick has no need to be ashamed. The policy of its leaders may not always have been beyond criticism, but their aims and interests have been elevated and unselfish. On the whole they have displayed both prudence and courage in dealing with difficulties, financial and administrative, and in the majority of cases they have successfully overcome them.

The Church, however, is not composed of its

leading men.  Much of its prosperity is also due to
the loyalty and generosity, the earnest prayers and
faithful service, of its undistinguished members.
That is not a true estimate of a Church of Christ
which regards chiefly its wealth, its culture, or
social standing.  These are well enough when they
are understood as gifts, and rightly subordinated to
spiritual ends.  The real strength and influence of a
church depend much more upon the due recognition
of all gifts, both great and small, and upon the consecration of every vessel, whether of gold or silver, of
wood or of earth, that it may be meet for the
Master's use.

> "All service ranks the same with God ;
> There is no last nor first."

Brunswick is a typical Nonconformist Church, and
its history is an illustration of what Voluntaryism
can accomplish.  It recognizes no master but the
Lord Jesus Christ.  Its ministers are priests as all
Christians are, and they claim to exercise no greater
function than that of being servants of all for
Christ's sake.  While it fulfils its part in promoting

the welfare of the State, it asks nothing from the
State but the right to carry on its mission. Throughout its existence it has been entirely self-supporting.
It is impossible to calculate, with any approach to
accuracy, the amount of money that has been
contributed in support of the various departments
of its work. The first cost of the premises was
about £11,500, and probably half as much again has
been spent in various improvements. Large sums
have been paid year by year in salaries, in interest
on borrowed money, and in contributions to Connexional and benevolent institutions. The collections
at the Sunday school anniversaries for the last sixty
years have amounted in the aggregate to £7,872. So
long as institutions like this can exist and flourish,
and not only maintain their own strength, but
establish and support weaker and dependent communities, so long will it be demonstrated that the
Church of Christ requires neither the control nor
the aid of the State in order that it may fulfil its
mission to the world.

What will be its future? Will the next sixty

years exhibit a record comparable with that of the past? "God buries His workmen," it is said, "but carries on His work," and in the broader aspect of the case that saying is undoubtedly true. God's work is always being carried on in some form or another, but whether to a man or a church shall be given the privilege of aiding its advance, will depend on two things: first, on the devotion with which they apply themselves to the work; and second, on their capacity to meet the changing circumstances and needs of the times as they arise. Fervour and spiritual-mindedness are good, nay, they are essential, in order to generate the enthusiasm needful for success; but none the less necessary are intelligence, alertness, tact, and judgment, that the enthusiasm may be wisely directed.

Such qualities were manifested by the fathers of the Church, or this great institution would never have survived the difficulties that it has had to encounter. And their children are not destitute of them. It is to them that I appeal. Let business ability be sanctified by prayer, let consecrated enthusiasm be guided by wise statesmanship, and there is nothing that will hinder the continued progress of this Church. It is a rich heritage upon which you have entered, built up by the toil and self-sacrifice of past generations, and sacred with the prayers and the faith of those who now inherit the promises. To lightly desert or squander it would be ingratitude of the basest character; to improve it, to adapt it to altered conditions, to add to it the strength and freshness of your own gifts, so as to win thereby new triumphs for Christ and mankind, will be the noblest tribute to their memory. To quote the hackneyed but true and stirring words of Lowell:—

> "New occasions teach new duties;
> Time makes ancient good uncouth;
> They must upward still and onward,
> Who would keep abreast of truth."

The times are strangely altered, and in many ways for the better, since Brunswick Church was founded. The causes which led to its formation have been to some extent, though not entirely, removed, and there is a greater manifestation of

P

unity in aim and effort · among the Methodist
communities than has ever been seen before. There
are however great perils and besetments threatening
the Free Churches of our land. Attempts more or
less disguised are being made to tamper with liberty
of conscience, and to weaken, if not destroy, the
position of Nonconformity. The baseless pretensions
of Sacerdotalism appear to be gaining ground, and
it might seem as if the battle of religious freedom
would have to be fought over again. That these
perils will be faced and their evils averted, I do not
doubt, but there is need that the young should be
informed and watchful in regard to them. The
questions of the future will be religious questions,
and they will be solved, not by party politicians, but
by Christian men and women.

Some years ago Neander, the great German
teacher, said, "I see before my countrymen a deep
abyss, but above it there shines a bright light. Is it
the dawn or is it the evening twilight?" The light
has grown brighter since he spoke. Christ has not
had His day, "it has only dawned, it will come by
and by."

# APPENDICES.

## Appendix A.

## Ministers and Officials of the Bury Circuit.

| Year. | Ministers. | Stewards. | Secretaries. |
|---|---|---|---|
| 1836 | | James Livesey, *Chairman.* | John Lord. |
| 1837 | *In Rochdale Circuit;* Joseph Handley resident in Bury. | Charles Bates, Wm. Austin. | |
| 1838 | | Charles Bates, Wm. Austin. | |
| 1839 | | Charles Bates, Wm. Austin. | |
| 1840 | J. B. Sheppard | John Randle, Edward Potts | Thomas Hacking. |
| 1841 | J. B. Sheppard | John Randle, Edward Potts. | |
| 1842 | J. B. Sheppard, R. Rutherford. | Edward Potts, Joseph Buckley. | |
| 1843 | David Rutherford | Edward Potts, Joseph Buckley. | |
| 1844 | J. Molineux, W. Middleton | Edward Potts, John Towers. | |
| 1845 | J. Molineux, W. Middleton. | Edward Potts, John Towers. | |
| 1846 | J. Molineux, E. Pearson | Edward Potts, John Towers. | |
| 1847 | W. H. Walker | Edward Potts, John Towers. | |
| 1848 | W. H. Walker. | Edward Potts, John Towers. | |
| 1849 | Joseph Townend | Edward Potts, John Towers. | |
| 1850 | Joseph Townend, E. W. Buckley | Edward Potts, John Towers. | |
| 1851 | J. Wesley Gilchrist | Edward Potts, John Towers. | |
| 1852 | John Mather | Joseph Hacking, John Towers. | |
| 1853 | John Mather | Jos. Hacking, Robt. Isherwood. | |
| 1854 | John Mather | Jos. Hacking, Robt. Isherwood. | |
| 1855 | John Peters | Jos. Hacking, Robt. Isherwood. | |
| 1856 | John Peters | Jos. Hacking, Robt. Isherwood. | |
| 1857 | Edwin Wright, W. Stott | Robt. Isherwood, Richard Lord | |
| 1858 | Edwin Wright, W. Stott. | Robt. Isherwood, Richard Lord | Samuel Cook. |
| 1859 | Edwin Wright, G. Lord | Robt. Isherwood, Richard Lord | Samuel Cook. |
| 1860 | J. Kendall, J. Walker | Robt. Isherwood, Richard Lord | John Stockdale. |
| 1861 | J. Kendall, H. M. Cuttell | Robt. Isherwood, Richard Lord | John Stockdale. |

| Year | | | |
|---|---|---|---|
| 1862 | J. Kendall, H. M. Cuttell | Robt. Isherwood, Richard Lord | John Stockdale. |
| 1863 | W. R. Brown, J. Shaw | Robt. Isherwood, Richard Lord | John Stockdale. |
| 1864 | W. R. Brown, J. Shaw | Robt. Isherwood. Richard Lord | John Stockdale. |
| 1865 | W. R Brown, J. T. Hodge | Richard Lord, John Stockdale | John Stockdale. |
| 1866 | C. Ogden, J. T. Hodge | Richard Lord, John Stockdale | John Stockdale. |
| 1867 | C. Ogden, O. Greenwood | Richard Lord, Richard Mills | John Stockdale. |
| 1868 | E. Browning, S. Sellars, G. Price | Richard Lord, Richard Mills | John Stockdale. |
| 1869 | E. Browning, S. Sellars, G. Price | Richard Lord, Richard Mills | John Stockdale. |
| 1870 | W. R. Sunnan, H. T. Chapman | Richard Lord, Richard Mills | John Stockdale. |
| 1871 | W. R. Sunnan, T. Ashcroft | Richard Lord, Isaac Smith | John Stockdale. |
| 1872 | W. R. Sunnan, T. Ashcroft | George Ormerod, Henry Brown | John Stockdale. |
| 1873 | W. R. Sunnan, T. Ashcroft | George Ormerod, Henry Brown | John Stockdale. |
| 1874 | J. Adcock, T. Ashcroft | George Ormerod, Henry Brown | John Stockdale. |
| 1875 | J. Adcock, H. Holgate | George Ormerod, Henry Brown | John Stockdale. |
| 1876 | R. D. Maud, H. Holgate | Henry Brown, Edmund Eccles | J. K. Lord. |
| 1877 | R. D. Maud, H. Holgate | Edmund Eccles, Joseph Welsby | J. K. Lord. |
| 1878 | A. Hands, P. Bennett | Edmund Eccles, Joseph Welsby | J. K. Lord. |
| 1879 | A. Hands, P. Bennett | Edmund Eccles, Joseph Welsby | J. K. Lord. |
| 1880 | A. Hands, P. Bennett | Edmund Eccles, Joseph Welsby | J. K. Lord. |
| 1881 | A. Hands, C. Bentley | Edmund Eccles, Joseph Welsby | J. K. Lord. |
| 1882 | J. Kendall, C. Bentley | Edmund Eccles, Joseph Welsby | J. K. Lord. |
| 1883 | J. Kendall, S. W. Hopkins | Joseph Welsby, J. H. Riley | J. K. Lord. |
| 1884 | J. Kendall, S. W. Hopkins | Joseph Welsby, J. H. Riley | J. K. Lord. |
| 1885 | T. W. Townend, S. W. Hopkins | John Ashworth, J. H. Lord | J. K. Lord. |
| 1886 | T. W. Townend, J. Mather, J. Taylor | John Ashworth, J. H. Lord | J. K. Lord. |
| 1887 | T. W. Townend, J. Mather, J. Taylor. | J. H. Lord, T. Ormerod | J. K. Lord. |
| 1888 | J. Percival, J. Mather, J. Taylor | J. H. Lord, T. Ormerod | J. K. Lord. |
| 1889 | J. Percival, S. Poad, J. W. Davis | J. H. Lord, T. Ormerod | J. K. Lord. |
| 1890 | J. Percival, S. Poad, J. H. Shaw | J. H. Lord, T. Ormerod | J. K. Lord. |
| 1891 | S. Poad, T. P. Dale, J. H. Shaw | J. H. Lord, C. Farrer | J. K. Lord. |
| 1892 | S. Poad, T. P. Dale | J. H. Lord, J. H. Riley | J. K. Lord. |
| 1893 | T. P. Dale, J. Taylor | J. H. Lord, J. H. Riley | J. K. Lord. |
| 1894 | T. P. Dale, J. Taylor | J. H. Lord, J. H. Riley | J. K. Lord. |
| 1895 | T. P. Dale, J. Taylor | J. H. Lord, J. H. Riley | J. K. Lord. |

## Appendix B.
### Original Trustees of Brunswick Chapel.

Samuel Smith
Daniel Smith.
Richard Lord.
William Wild.
Samuel Cook.
Robert Isherwood.
Robert Bleasdale.
Robert Hall.
William Leach Blomley.

George Lord Ashworth.
William Tuer.
John Petrie.
William Robinson.
James Buckley.
Joseph Hacking.
George Stockdale.
Joseph Burgoine.
John Fishwick.

Though not at the time declared trustees by a duly executed trust deed, the following brethren, in conjunction with the surviving members of the original body of trustees, were, for a considerable period, entrusted with the management of the Trust Estate, viz. : — George Ormerod, Thomas Ormerod, Henry Brown, John Burgoine, John Kay Lord, James Ashworth, Jesse Meadowcroft, Edmund Eccles, Benjamin Moorhouse, Henry Moorhouse, James Jopson, Lambert Fletcher, Joseph Welsby, Samuel Smith, Edwin Smith, John Ashworth, Handel Ashworth, Abel Ashworth, J. H. Riley, C. Talbot, R. Jackson, J. H. Lord, William Stockdale, Benjamin Bolton, E. Burgoine.

Joseph Clemishaw, though his name does not appear in the foregoing list, rendered important service for some years, as Secretary to the Trustees.

### List of Trustees appointed under the last deed, completed November, 1885.

*Richard Lord.*
*William Wild.*
*George L. Ashworth.*
*James Ashworth.*
John Ashworth.
Thomas Ashworth.
Handel Ashworth.
John R. Barnes.
Thomas Brown.
*Samuel Butterworth.*
Edmund Eccles.
Lambert Fletcher.
Mark Hargreaves.
*James Jopson.*
Robert Jackson
John Kay Lord.
John Henry Lord.

William Lord.
Jesse Meadowcroft.
Benjamin Moorhouse.
Thomas Ormerod.
Joseph H. Riley.
William Roberts.
John Smith.
E. W. B. Smith.
William W. Standring.
John Taylor.
Christopher Talbot.
*Joseph Robinson.*
*Joseph Welsby.*
*George Wensley.*
John Wolstenholme.
James Holt, *Secretary.*
The Superintendent Minister.

Those whose names are printed in italics are deceased.

Mr. Samuel Smith has retained the office of Treasurer to the Trust since the death of his father, in 1869.

## Appendix C.

## Superintendents of Brunswick Sunday School.

| Year. | Boys' Side. | Girls' Side. |
|---|---|---|
| January, 1836 | John Clemishaw (the only name to be traced). | Henry Holden, J. Mills, J. Kay. |
| July, 1837 | R. Collins, R. Bleasdale, S. Smith | J. Bolton, J. Randle, R. Collins. |
| January, 1837 | J. Buckley, J. Barker, R. Isherwood | J. Clemishaw, H. Holden, S. Smith. |
| January, 1838 | C. Bates, J. Buckley, W. Isherwood | J. Clemishaw, H. Holden, S. Smith. |
| July, 1838 | C. Bates, Abel Ashworth, J. Randle | William Isherwood. |
| January, 1839 | James Buckley | James Buckley. |
| July, 1839 | Samuel Smith | William Tuer. |
| January, 1840 | Charles Bates | William Tuer. |
| July, 1840 | Charles Bates | William Tuer. |
| January, 1841 | Charles Bates | James Fletcher. |
| July, 1841 | James Buckley | James Fletcher. |
| January, 1842 | James Buckley | James Fletcher. |
| July, 1842 | James Buckley | George Lord Ashworth. |
| January, 1843 | Thomas Haslegraves | Robert Hall. |
| July, 1843 | G. L. Ashworth | Richard Lord. |
| January, 1844 | William Tuer | Richard Lord. |
| July, 1844 | James Buckley | Richard Lord. |
| January, 1845 | James Buckley | Richard Lord. |
| July, 1845 | James Buckley | William Tuer. |
| January, 1846 | James Buckley | Samuel Cook. |
| July, 1846 | John Dearden | John Dearden, Robert Bleasdale. |
| | *Alteration of Rules.* | |
| October, 1846 | G. L. Ashworth, Samuel Cook | Robert Bleasdale, G. L. Ashworth |
| July, 1847 | Samuel Cook, Samuel Smith | Joshua Lord, William Moorhouse. |
| January, 1848 | Joseph Hacking, Robert Hall... | |

| YEAR. | BOYS' SIDE. | GIRLS' SIDE. |
|---|---|---|
| July, 1848 | — | Robert Hall, William Moorhouse. |
| January, 1849 | *No record.* | Robert Hall, William Moorhouse, |
| July, 1849 | Samuel Cook, Joshua Lord ... ... | William Moorhouse, Samuel Smith. |
| January, 1850 | James Riley, Richard Lord ... ... | William Moorhouse, Samuel Smith. |
| July, 1850 | James Riley, Richard Lord ... ... | William Moorhouse, John Willis. |
| January, 1851 | Richard Lord, Joseph Hacking ... ... | William Moorhouse, John Willis. |
| July, 1851 | Richard Lord, Joseph Hacking ... | John Willis, Joseph Fletcher. |
| January, 1852 | Samuel Smith, G. L. Ashworth ... | John Willis, Joseph Fletcher. |
| July, 1852 | Samuel Smith, G. L. Ashworth ... | John Willis, Joseph Fletcher. |
| January, 1853 | Samuel Smith, G. L. Ashworth ... | John Willis, Joseph Fletcher. |
| July, 1853 | Samuel Smith, John Ormerod ... | John Willis, Joseph Fletcher. |
| January, 1854 | Samuel Smith, John Ormerod ... | John Willis, Joseph Fletcher. |
| July, 1854 | Samuel Smith, John Ormerod ... | John Willis, Joseph Fletcher. |
| January, 1855 | Samuel Smith, John Ormerod ... | John Willis, Joseph Fletcher. |
| July, 1855 | Samuel Smith, John Ormerod ... | John Willis, Joseph Fletcher. |
| January, 1856 | Samuel Smith, Isaac Smith ... | John Willis, Peter Smith. |
| July, 1856 | Samuel Smith, Isaac Smith ... | John Willis, Peter Smith. |
| | Samuel Smith, Isaac Smith ... | John Willis, Peter Smith. |
| | *Record lost until the following date.* | |
| July, 1861 | John Stockdale, Isaac Smith ... | Peter Smith, James Ashworth. |
| January, 1862 | John Stockdale, Isaac Smith ... | Peter Smith, James Ashworth. |
| July, 1862 | John Stockdale, Isaac Smith ... | Peter Smith, James Ashworth. |
| January, 1863 | John Stockdale, John Collins ... | Peter Smith, James Ashworth. |
| July, 1863 | James Jopson, George Ormerod ... | Peter Smith, James Ashworth. |
| January, 1864 | James Jopson, George Ormerod ... | Peter Smith, James Ashworth. |
| July, 1864 | James Jopson, George Ormerod ... | Peter Smith, James Ashworth. |
| January, 1865 | James Jopson, George Ormerod ... | Peter Smith, James Ashworth. |

| Date | | |
|---|---|---|
| July, 1865 | James Jopson, John Collins ... | James Ashworth, Lambert Fletcher. |
| July, 1866 | James Jopson, John Collins ... | James Ashworth, Lambert Fletcher. |
| July, 1867 | James Jopson, Isaac Smith | James Ashworth, Lambert Fletcher. |
| July, 1868 | James Jopson, John Collins ... | James Ashworth, Lambert Fletcher. |
| July, 1869 | James Jopson, John Collins ... | William Eagle, Lambert Fletcher. |
| July, 1870 | James Jopson, John Collins ... | William Eagle, Lambert Fletcher. |
| July, 1871 | Isaac Smith, John Collins ... | William Eagle, Lambert Fletcher. |
| July, 1872 | Isaac Smith, Thomas Ormerod | William Eagle, Lambert Fletcher. |
| January, 1873 | John Collins, Thomas Ormerod | William Eagle, Lambert Fletcher. |
| January, 1874 | John Collins, William Eagle ... | Lambert Fletcher, Robert Jackson. |
| January, 1875 | John Ashworth ... | Robert Jackson. |
| January, 1876 | John Ashworth ... | Robert Jackson. |
| January, 1877 | John Smith ... | John Ashworth. |
| January, 1878 | George Ormerod, Robert Jackson | Thomas Ormerod, William Roberts. |
| January, 1879 | Robert Jackson, Cornelius Farrer... | Thomas Ormerod, John Ashworth. |
| January, 1880 | Robert Jackson, Lambert Fletcher | Thomas Ormerod, J. H. Riley. |
| January, 1881 | Lambert Fletcher ... | J. H. Riley. |
| January, 1882 | William Stockdale ... | J. H. Riley. |
| January, 1883 | William Stockdale, James Holt ... | J. H. Riley. |
| January, 1884 | Thomas Ormerod ... | J. H. Riley. |
| January, 1885 | John Ashworth ... | J. H. Riley. |
| January, 1886 | John Ashworth ... | James Holt. |
| January, 1887 | John Ashworth ... | James Holt. |
| January, 1888 | Thomas Ormerod ... | James Holt. |
| January, 1889 | James Holt ... | J. H. Riley. |
| January, 1890 | James Holt ... | J. H. Riley. |
| January, 1891 | James Holt ... | J. H. Riley. |
| January, 1892 | James Holt ... | J. H. Riley. |
| January, 1893 | James Holt ... | J. H. Riley. |
| January, 1894 | James Holt ... | Lambert Fletcher. |
| January, 1895 | E. W. B. Smith ... | Lambert Fletcher. |
| January, 1896 | James Willis ... | Lambert Fletcher. |

## School Anniversary Services. Names of Preachers and Amount of Collections.

| Year. | Morning. | Afternoon. | Evening. | £ | s. | d. |
|---|---|---|---|---|---|---|
| 1836 | Mr. Wm. Aldred. | Rev. Mr. Mackey. | Rev. J. Peters. | 107 | 13 | 1 |
| 1837 | Rev. J. Wolstenholme. | Rev. J. H. Roebuck. | Rev. Dr. Warren. | 91 | 7 | 1 |
| 1838 | Rev. J. Molineux. | Mr. D. Rowland. | Rev. J. Molineux. | 69 | 12 | 9 |
| 1839 | Rev. Mr. Mackey. | Rev. H. Breeden. | Rev. H. Breeden. | 71 | 1 | 10½ |
| 1840 | Rev. J. Molineux. | Rev. W. Dawson. | Rev. Mr. Mackey. | 45 | 6 | 3 |
| 1841 | Rev. J. Molineux. | Rev. J. Peters. | Rev. J. Molineux. | 42 | 6 | 2 |
| 1842 | Rev. J. Molineux. | Rev. W. Ince. | Rev. J. Molineux. | 42 | 2 | 9 |
| 1843 | Rev. J. Wolstenholme. | Rev. J. Wolstenholme. | Rev. W. McKerrow. | 49 | 14 | 7½ |
| 1844 | Rev. W. Dawson. | Rev. H. Breeden. | Rev. W. Dawson. | 50 | 2 | 10 |
| 1845 | Rev. J. Molineux. | Rev. W. Middleton. | Rev. J. Molineux. | 44 | 6 | 6½ |
| 1846 | Rev. J. Molineux. | Rev. J. Peters. | Rev. J. Peters. | 59 | 6 | 7 |
| 1847 | Rev. Jos. Saul. | Rev. E. Pearson. | Rev. Jos. Saul. | 50 | 8 | 11½ |
| 1848 | Rev. W. H. Walker. | Rev. W. H. Walker. | Rev. W. R. Thorburn. | 44 | 0 | 10½ |
| 1849 | Rev. J. Molineux. | Rev. J. Guttridge. | Rev. J. Molineux. | 60 | 1 | 0¾ |
| 1850 | Rev. J. Townend. | Rev. A. Weston. | Rev. J. Townend. | 60 | 5 | 10 |
| 1851 | Rev. J. Townend. | Rev. J. Townend. | Rev. J. Townend. | 72 | 8 | 2½ |
| 1852 | Rev. J. Guttridge. | Rev. J. Guttridge. | Rev. J. W. Gilchrist. | 57 | 0 | 5½ |
| 1853 | Mr. Wilson. | Rev. J. Mather. | Rev. J. Mather. | 66 | 2 | 11½ |
| 1854 | Rev. J. Molineux. | Rev. S. S. Barton. | Rev. S. S. Barton. | 65 | 0 | 11½ |
| 1855 | Rev. J. Molineux. | Rev. J. Mather. | Rev. J. Mather. | 61 | 9 | 4 |
| 1856 | Mr. J. Ashworth. | Rev. J. Peters. | Rev. J. Peters. | 62 | 11 | 6 |
| 1857 | Mr. J. Ashworth. | Rev. W. Beckett. | Rev. W. Beckett. | 68 | 3 | 8 |
| 1858 | Mr. Wright. | Rev. W. Stott. | Rev. E. Wright. | 78 | 5 | 5 |
| 1859 | Mr. B. Fothergill. | Rev. John Steele. | Rev. John Steele. | 72 | 5 | 2½ |
| 1860 | Rev. J. Molineux. | Rev. R. Chew. | Rev. R. Chew. | 74 | 11 | 6 |
| 1861 | Mr. J. Ashworth. | Rev. J. Kendall. | Rev. J. Kendall. | 71 | 17 | 11½ |

| Year | | | | | | |
|---|---|---|---|---|---|---|
| 1862 | Mr. J. Ashworth. | Rev. M. Miller. | Rev. M. Miller. | 80 | 16 | 4½ |
| 1863 | Mr. J. Ashworth. | Rev. J. Mather. | Rev. J. Mather. | 81 | 10 | 5 |
| 1864 | Mr. J. Ashworth. | Rev. J. Shaw. | Rev. W. R. Brown. | 83 | 5 | 4 |
| 1865 | Mr. J. Ashworth. | Rev. J. S. Withington. | Rev. J. S. Withington. | 112 | 5 | 5¼ |
| 1866 | Mr. J. Ashworth. | Rev. W. Griffith. | Rev. W. Griffith. | 128 | 13 | 9 |
| 1867 | Mr. J. Ashworth. | Rev. J. Townend. | Rev. C. Ogden. | 161 | 4 | 0½ |
| 1868 | Mr. J. Ashworth. | Rev. A. Hands. | Rev. C. Ogden. | 160 | 0 | 6½ |
| 1869 | Mr. J. Ashworth. | Rev. S. Sellars. | Rev. E. Browning. | 159 | 7 | 5½ |
| 1870 | Mr. J. Ashworth. | Rev. C. Ogden. | Rev. C. Ogden. | 155 | 4 | 1 |
| 1871 | Mr. J. Ashworth. | Rev. W. R. Sunman. | Rev. W. R. Sunman. | 202 | 8 | 4 |
| 1872 | Mr. J. Ashworth. | Rev. W. R. Sunman. | Rev. T. Ashcroft. | 206 | 13 | 2½ |
| 1873 | Mr. Wm. Sunman. | Rev. T. Ashcroft. | Rev. W. R. Sunman. | 195 | 7 | 8½ |
| 1874 | Mr. J. Ashworth. | Rev. J. Kendall. | Rev. J. Kendall. | 190 | 15 | 9½ |
| 1875 | Mr. J. Harley. | Rev. J. Adcock. | Rev. J. Adcock. | 207 | 10 | 4½ |
| 1876 | Mr. J. Harley. | Rev. J. Adcock. | Rev. H. Holgate. | 211 | 12 | 4½ |
| 1877 | Rev. J. Adcock. | Rev. J. Adcock. | Rev. R. D. Maud. | 219 | 8 | 11¼ |
| 1878 | Rev. R. Grey. | Rev. T. M. Booth. | Rev. T. M. Booth. | 202 | 11 | 7½ |
| 1879 | Rev. A. Hands. | Rev. A. Hands. | Rev. P. Bennett. | 200 | 5 | 10 |
| 1880 | Rev. J. Mather. | Rev. J. Mather. | Rev. A. Hands. | 195 | 8 | 3½ |
| 1881 | Rev. W. O. Lilley. | Rev. T. B. Saul. | Rev. T. B. Saul. | 191 | 18 | 1 |
| 1882 | Rev. W. R. Sunman. | Rev. W. R. Sunman. | Rev. C. Bentley. | 209 | 14 | 0½ |
| 1883 | Rev. S. K. Hocking. | Rev. S. K. Hocking. | Rev. J. Kendall. | 180 | 15 | 3 |
| 1884 | Mr. A. Alsop. | Rev. A. Holliday. | Rev. S. W. Hopkins. | 201 | 0 | 10 |
| 1885 | Rev. W. R. Sunman. | Rev. J. F. Broughton. | Rev. W. R. Sunman. | 200 | 7 | 9½ |
| 1886 | Rev. F. Bavin. | Rev. F. Bavin. | Rev. T. W. Townend. | 201 | 14 | 2½ |
| 1887 | Rev. W. Stott. | Rev. W. Stott. | Rev. I. Taylor. | 201 | 15 | 0½ |
| 1888 | Rev. B. J. Tungate. | Rev. B. J. Tungate. | Rev. B. J. Tungate. | 200 | 1 | 7 |
| 1889 | Rev. R. Abercrombie, M.A. | Rev. R. Abercrombie, M.A. | Rev. J. Percival. | 200 | 16 | 0 |
| 1890 | Mr. L. K. Shaw. | Rev. E. Evans. | Rev. J. Percival. | 193 | 18 | 0 |
| 1891 | Rev. S. K. Hocking. | Rev. S. K. Hocking. | Rev. J. Mather. | 191 | 0 | 2 |
| 1892 | Rev. E. Evans. | Rev. S. Foad. | Rev. T. P. Dale. | 180 | 0 | 5 |
| 1893 | Rev. R. Chew. | Rev. R. Chew. | Rev. T. P. Dale. | 179 | 15 | 8 |
| 1894 | Mr. J. Duckworth. | Rev. W. R. Sunman. | Rev. W. R. Sunman. | 168 | 18 | 9 |
| 1895 | Mr. J. E. Balmer. | Rev. J. Adcock. | Rev. J. Adcock. | 187 | 6 | 5 |
| 1896 | Rev. W. Barnes. | Rev. J. Hocking. | Rev. J. Hocking. | 191 | 7 | 2 |

# APPENDIX E.

## LIST OF SINGERS AT THE ANNIVERSARY OF 1872.

Organist - - - MR. EDWIN SMITH.
Conductor - - - MR. JESSE MEADOWCROFT.

### TREBLE.

Martha Cockshott
Emma Talbot
Elizabeth Ann Talbot
Sarah Whittaker
Amelia Platt
Lizzie Wood
Alice Wood
Hannah Bertwistle
Ruth Taylor
Elizabeth Ann Fletcher
Mary Ann Robinson
Alice Robinson
Ellen Huddlestone
Alice Wolstenholme
Sarah Jane Taylor
Mary Diggle
Emma Chadwick
Elizabeth Wolstenholme
Maria Wood
Sarah Mellor
Rachel Howard
Margaret Duckworth
Mary Jane Hope
Mary Ellen Brown
Elizabeth Ann Hill
Mary Jane Wild
Deborah Wild
Mary Ann Wilkinson
Louisa Turner
Mary Jane Platt
Emma Hall
Sarah Pickup
Maria Stout
Alice Taylor
Eliza Diggle
Alice Mills
Sarah Ann Eccles
Mary Tinsley
Rachel Tomlinson

Jane Humphrey
Hannah Bridge
Mary Hook
Elizabeth Whittaker
Sarah Ann Ashworth
Susannah Coop
Margaret Ann Dawson
Elizabeth Ann Hall
Mary Jane Jones
Sarah Alice Rigby
Elizabeth Ann Hill
Jane Wild
Sarah Ann Blomeley
Florence Mills
Matilda Bertwistle
Mary Jane Burgoine
Mary Ellen Brown
Alice Ann Settle
Mary Alice Bowker
Mary Holt
Eliza Talbot
Betsy Jowett
Sarah Butterworth
Elizabeth J. Huddlestone
Sarah Chadwick
Elizabeth Ann Clegg
Mary Ellen Grundy
Elizabeth Turner
Martha Ellen Holt
Mary Alice Bickerstaffe
Elizabeth Blomeley
Annie Griffiths
Alice Fletcher
Sarah Alice Pickles
Sarah Maria Barlow
Harriet Suthurst
Nancy Suthurst
Sarah Jane Suthurst
Alice Mills
Margaret Ann Ormerod

Eliza Jackson
Mary Ellen Stock
Eliza Ann Makin
Alice Atherton
Martha Ann Kershaw
Ann Walker
Mary Nuttall
Margaret Ellen Walker
Margaret Smith
Sarah Barlow
Esther Green
Ellen Heyworth
Alice Varley
Mary Jane Bell
Dinah Mills
Bertha Coulthurst
Eliza Openshaw
Mary Jane Yates
Henrietta Brown
Mary Allen
Emma Fletcher
Mary Shaw
Hannah Ellen Porter
Sarah Ann Barlow
Alice Wood
Sarah Alice Ashworth
Ellen Maxwell
Susannah Booth
Sarah Taylor
Emma Kay
Mary Ellen Greenhalgh
Sarah Whitehead
Ellen Marsden
Elizabeth Ann Marsden
Jane Rhodes
Florence Brown
Jane Wolstenholme
Betsy Hannah Hamilton
Mary Alice Barton
Alice Ann Settle

M. A. Fletcher Moorhouse
Mary Ann Bainbridge
Isabella Greaves
Elizabeth Grundy
Mary Ellen Butterworth
Elizabeth Jane Marshall
Mary Alice Walker
Sarah Farnworth
Maria Dawson
Sarah Chadwick
Ann Whitehead
Mary Jane Green
Fanny Fletcher
Ellen Allen
Alice Fletcher
Mary Ellen Grundy
Elizabeth Alice Clegg
Mary Alice Barlow
Frances Wild
Ann Wild
Elizabeth Barton
Sarah Heys
Catherine Bainbridge
Elizabeth Heyworth
Selina Warburton
Eliza Heyworth
Clara Suthurst
Eliza Whittam
Sarah Alice Rigby
Mary Jane Jones
Hannah Hill
Mary Ann Crawshaw
Nancy Duckworth
Sarah Ann Walker
Tabitha Nuttall
Sarah Jane Suthurst
Sarah Fishwick
Mary Ann Fenton
Eliza Fenton
Sarah Holt
Sarah Smith
Sarah Mitchell
Martha Ellen Varley
Alice Farnworth
Rachel Hamilton
Clara Fletcher
Dinah Wilkinson
Elizabeth Hacking
Ellen Farnworth

Elizabeth Jones
Amelia Jones
Annie Chaffer
Annie Mills
Epshaw Hartley

## ALTO.

Elizabeth Beckett
Sarah Jane Hall
Mary Wood
Mary Ann Tomlinson
Hannah Reed
Alice Taylor
Nelson Booth
William Talbot
William A. Platt
Jesse Varley
Wilbraim Dawson
David Fletcher
Phineas Fletcher
Alfred Platt
Thomas Moorhouse
Thomas P. Fletcher
Thomas Bainbridge
Handel Fletcher
Harry Gill
William Chaffer
Walter Taylor
Richard Norris Taylor
Walter Brown
Edward Brown
John Dawson
Josiah Jackson
Alfred Spragg
George Pollitt
William Newbold
John Openshaw
James Mitchell
Edwin P. Crisp
William Hardman
Walter Greenhalgh
Elias Sanderson
John Allen
Samuel Forshaw
Robert Whittaker
John Henry Howarth
James Whitworth
Peter Smith
Thomas Warbrick

John Smith
Thomas Allen
Thomas Edward Tinsley
Thomas Wolstenholme
James Mitchell

## TENOR.

Robert Ormerod
Thomas Rigby
Thomas Hibbert
Thomas Platt
Theophilus Talbot
James Henry Wild
Joseph Allen
William Clemishaw
Henry Duckworth
Edward Kempster
William Wild
William Barlow
William Grime
John Whittaker
Parmenus Coulthurst
Joseph Reed
William Sharp
Joseph Green

## BASS.

John Reed
Peter Allen
Peter Smith
Robert Hardman
William Lightbown
Edwin Harold Wilcock
Josiah Grisdale
James Reed
James Holt
William Holt
Edward Standring
William Coulthurst
Robert Cooper
Joseph Clifton
Christopher Jackson
Joseph Chadwick
Roger Peel
James Wood
James Bracewell
Joseph Albiston
Joseph Fletcher
William Lomax
William Bradbury

## DATES AND EVENTS.

1703    John Wesley born, June 17.

1774    Wesley's first visit to Bury, and Opening of New Meeting House at Pits o'th Moor, April 16.

1778    Wesley's last visit to Bury, December 12.

1791    John Wesley died, March 2.

1804    Bury became a Circuit.

1815    Union Street Chapel built.

1835    Meeting at Bolton Street Chapel, April 10.
Delegate Meeting at Manchester, April 25.
Dr. Warren expelled from Wesleyan Conference, July 29.
Withdrawal of James Livesey in Bury, October 9.
Meeting at Bethel Chapel, October 17.

1836    Secession from Clerke Street School, January 10
Sick and Burial Society established, February 21
First School Sermons, May 22.
Corner Stone of Old Brunswick Chapel, May 27.
United to Rochdale Circuit, September.

1837    First Interment at Brunswick, February 6.
Brunswick Old Chapel opened, March 24.
Second School Sermons, June 10.
James Livesey President, August 2.
Dorcas Society begun, October 21.

1840    The Bury Circuit formed, August.

1842    Bolton Refugees joined, February.

1847   Bury and Bolton Circuit divided, August.

1849   Brunswick Temperance Society established, January 28.

1850   Visit of Connexional Committee, November.

1851   Foundation Stone of Heap Bridge Chapel laid, August 6.
      New Settlement of Property, September.
      Heap Bridge Old Chapel opened, December 25.

1852   Brunswick Chapel beautified and re-opened, September 5.

1855   Limefield Chapel opened, December 9.
      Organ opened in Brunswick, December 27.

1860   School Missionary appointed.

1861   Bazaar in the Athenæum, May 8.

1862   Corner Stone of New Chapel laid, June 14.

1864   Opening of Brunswick New Chapel, December 7.
      Mount Tabor Chapel, Birtle, opened.

1866   Foundation Stone of Elton Chapel laid, Whit-Friday.
      Corner Stone of Heap Bridge New Chapel, November, 3.

1867   Elton Chapel opened, October 17.

1838   Heap Bridge New Chapel opened, April

1869   Brunswick Chapel beautified and re-opened, October 14.
      Corner Stone of Warth Chapel laid, August 1.

1870   Brunswick Infant School commenced, January.
      Warth Chapel opened, February 16.

1871   Brunswick mixed Day School commenced, January.
       Ramsbottom Circuit formed, August.

1879   Brunswick Chapel Roof gave way, April.
       Brunswick Chapel re-opened, October 7.

1881   Robert Hall, Mayor.

1882   Great Bazaar opened, October 18.

1883   Foundation Stones of Parkhills School laid, June 2.
       Parkhills School opened, November 11.

1886   Adult Bible Class established, January.
       Brunswick Jubilee celebrated, April 23.

1891   Sale of Work for New Organ Fund, March 18.

1892   New Organ opened.

1893   John Ashworth, Mayor.
       Visit of Foreign Missionary Committee, June.

1894   Christian Endeavour Society commenced, June 6.

1895   Visit of Connexional Committee, October.

FLETCHER AND SPEIGHT, PRINTERS, BURY,

www.ingramcontent.com/pod-product-compliance
Lightning Source LLC
Chambersburg PA
CBHW020850270326
41928CB00006B/641